Grade Six

Music Theory

(ABRSM Syllabus)

GRADE SIX MUSIC THEORY COURSE AND EXERCISES

By Victoria Williams

www.mymusictheory.com

Copyright © 2016 Victoria Williams

All rights reserved.

1st Edition

ISBN-13: 978-1530907298

ISBN-10: 1530907292

CONTENTS

Introduction	8
A1 Introduction to Harmony	9
A2 Triads and Chords	11
A2 Triads and Chords Exercises	14
A2 Triads and Chords Answers	15
A3 Inversions	16
A3 Inversions Exercises	18
A3 Inversions Answers	19
A4 Chord Progressions	20
A4 Chord Progressions Exercises	26
A4 Chord Progression Answers	28
A5 Melodic Decoration	29
A5 Melodic Decoration Exercises	34
A5 Melodic Decoration Answers	36
A6 Harmonising a Melody I	37
A7 Harmonising a Melody II	42
A6 & A7 Harmonising a Melody Exercises	46
A6 & A7 Harmonizing a Melody Answers	48
A8 Introduction to Figured Bass	50
A8 Introduction to Figured Bass Exercises	56
A8 Introduction to Figured Bass Answers	57
A9 Figured Bass Rules	58
A9 Figured Bass Rules Exercises	61
A9 Figured Bass Rules Answers	63
A10 Figured Bass Realisation	64
A10 Figured Bass Realisation Exercises	69
A10 Figured Bass Realisation Answers	70
A11 Adding a Figured Bass line	71
A11 Adding a Figured Bass Line Exercises	76
A11 Adding a Figured Bass Line Answers	77
B Grade 6 Composition - Introduction	78
B1 Architecture	79

B1 Architecture Exercises 83

B1 Architecture Answers 85

B2 Motifs & Sequences 86

B2 Motifs and Sequences Exercises 91

B2 Motifs and Sequences Answers 94

B3 Cadences 97

B3 Cadences Exercises 100

B3 Cadences Answers 102

B4 Interpolation 103

B4 Interpolation Exercises 106

B4 Interpolation Answers 107

B5 Key and Tonality 108

B5 Key and Tonality Exercises 111

B5 Key and Tonality Answers 113

B6 Modulation 114

B6 Modulation Exercises 119

B6 Modulation Answers 121

B7 How to Compose 122

B7 Composing Exercises 128

B7 Composing Answers 131

C1a Reading an Orchestral Score 133

C1a Reading an Orchestral Score Exercises 138

C1a Reading an Orchestral Score Answers 140

C1b Reading a Chamber Music Score 141

C1b Reading a Chamber Music Score Exercises 144

C1b Reading a Chamber Music Score Answers 146

C2a Instruments, Families and Names 147

C2a Instruments, Families and Names Exercises 150

C2a Instruments, Families and Names Answers 152

C2b Transposing, String and Reed Instruments 153

C2b Transposing, String and Reed Exercises 155

C2b Transposing, String and Reeds Answers 157

C3 Musical Terms and Signs 158

C3 Musical Terms and Signs Exercises 163

C3 Musical Terms and Signs Answers 165

C4 Commenting on Music 166

C4 Commenting on Music Exercises 171

C4 Commenting on Music Answers 175

C5 Key 176

C5 Key Exercises 181

C5 Key Answers 187

C6a Naming Chords 188

C6b Chords in a Score 191

C6 Naming Chords Exercises 194

C6 Naming Chords Answers 198

C7a Ornaments 199

C7a Ornaments Exercises 203

C7a Ornaments Answers 206

C7b Melodic Decoration and Pedals 209

C7b Melodic Decoration and Pedals Exercises 211

C7b Melodic Decoration and Pedals Answers 213

C8 Technical Tasks 214

C8 Technical Tasks Exercises 217

C8 Technical Tasks Answers 222

C9 Periods and Composers 223

C9 Periods and Composers Exercises 232

C9 Periods and Composers Answers 238

INTRODUCTION

This book was written for students who are preparing to take the ABRSM Grade Six Music Theory exam. Parents of younger students will also find it helpful, as well as busy music teachers who are trying to fit a lot of music theory teaching into a very short time during instrumental lessons.

Each topic is broken down into digestible steps, and for best results the lessons should be followed in the order they are presented, as the acquired knowledge is cumulative.

After each topic, you will find a page or so of practice exercises, to help you consolidate what you have learned. Answers are provided on the page following the exercises.

I also highly recommend purchasing ABRSM past papers before sitting an actual exam. These can be obtained from shop.abrsm.org, Amazon or your local sheet music reseller.

You are welcome to photocopy the pages of this book for your own use, or to use with your pupils if you are a music teacher.

ABOUT THE AUTHOR

Victoria Williams graduated with a BA Hons degree in Music from the University of Leeds, UK, in 1995, where she specialised in notation and musicology.

In 2007 she decided to open up music theory teaching to a worldwide platform, by creating www.mymusictheory.com, which initially offered free lessons for Grade 5 ABRSM Music Theory candidates. Over the years, the full spectrum of ABRSM theory grades has been added, making MyMusicTheory one of the only websites worldwide offering a comprehensive, free, music theory training programme aligned with the ABRSM syllabuses.

You can connect with Victoria Williams in the following ways:

www.mymusictheory.com

info@mymusictheory.com

www.facebook.com/mymusictheory

www.twitter.com/mymusictheory

https://www.youtube.com/user/musictheoryexpert

A1 INTRODUCTION TO HARMONY

What is harmony? The first three questions in the ABRSM grade six music theory exam are all about **harmony** - but what exactly do we mean by "harmony"? When we look at music with our analytical hats on, we can think about it in two different ways. We can look at it from left to right - this is the **melody** and **rhythm**. Or, we can look at it from top to bottom - this is the **harmony**.

For example, here are a few bars by Bach from his "*O haupt voll Blut und Wunden*". There are 4 melodic lines (or "voices") here, the soprano, alto, tenor and bass.

Soprano:

Alto:

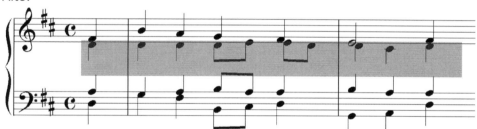

Tenor:

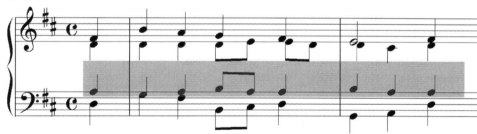

Bass:

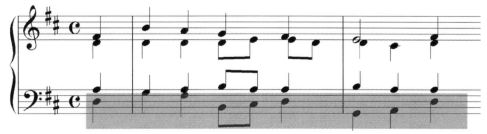

On each beat of the bar, those four voices combine to make chords. The science of how we combine notes into chords, and how the chords work together, is called "harmony".

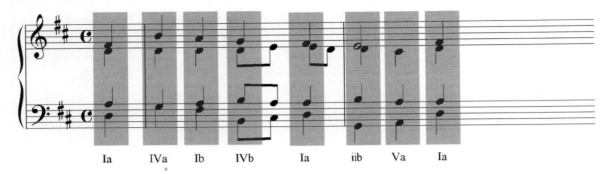

(Note that some chords above have been simplified).

Tonal Harmony

For Grade 6, we are going to study **tonal harmony.** This just means that we're going to focus on the kinds of chords used by composers from roughly the 17th to the 19th centuries - composers like Bach, Mozart, Haydn and Schubert.

Grade Six Harmony

In this part of the course we're going to study:

- How chords are built
- Different naming systems to describe chords
- Chord inversions
- Chord progressions and cadences
- How to choose chords to harmonise a melody (Q.1a in the exam)
- How to understand "figured bass" (which is a chord short-hand system)
- How to complete a bass line and add a suitable figured bass (Q.1b in the exam)
- How to recognise "melodic decoration" (which means notes which aren't part of the main chords)
- How to realise a figured bass (Q.2 in the exam)

A2 TRIADS AND CHORDS

A chord is any group of notes which are played at the same time.

Chords can have any number of notes in them, as long as there is more than one!

Chords can have any combination of notes in them, but our ears usually prefer listening to chords which are built to the rules of harmony, rather than just a random selection of notes.

These chords are built according to the rules of "tonal harmony". (Don't worry about the names of the chords for now!)

C major   G minor   C# dim 7th   French 6th

Whereas these chords were created by my cat walking across my piano keyboard (he's never studied harmony).

As we just saw, chords built using the rules of tonal harmony have **names**. There are a few different methods we can use to describe chords in words, and we'll take a look at these shortly. Before that, we'll go back to the basics of how to build chords in tonal harmony - using **triads**.

TRIADS

A triad is a 3-note chord. Take a note (call it the "root"), add a third and a fifth above it, and you have created a triad. (All triads are chords, but not all chords are triads.)

Take a note: We'll take an F:

Add a major third above it:

or a minor third:

Add a fifth above it to make a **major triad**:

or a **minor triad**:

We can also build a triad with a minor 3rd and a **diminished** 5th, like this:

This is called a **diminished triad**.

Scales and Triads

Each scale has a series of triads built from each degree of the scale.

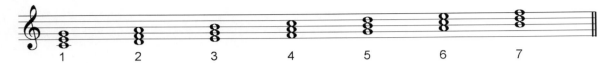

Look at each degree of the major scale and see if it produces a **major**, **minor** or **diminished** triad.

	1	2	3	4	5	6	7
	major	minor	minor	major	major	minor	diminished

This pattern is the same for all major keys.

Let's do the same with a minor scale. We normally use the harmonic (not melodic) variety of the scale to work out triads in music theory. Here's the group of triads which exist in A minor:

	1	2	3	4	5	6	7
	minor	diminished	augmented	minor	major	major	diminished

Watch out! Chord 3 is an **augmented** triad- rarely used in practice. It has an augmented 5th between the root and 5th. However, you may also see a **major** chord III (e.g. C major in this case) and also a **major** chord VII (G major in this case) – because these two chords are the same as the **relative major** key tonic (C major) and dominant (G major).

Naming Triads

Here are three methods we can use to name triads:

1. We can use the **letter name of the root** of the triad, and then add either "major", "minor" or "diminished" (or "augmented") to it.

E.g. C major (or just "C" for short), E minor (or "Em") and B diminished ("B dim").

2. We can use **Roman numerals**. Each degree of the scale gets a Roman numeral. We use capitals for major, lower case letters for minor, and lower case with a small circle ° for diminished. (Augmented chords are written in capitals with a + sign, but we don't use them in grade 6.)

Major Scales:

1	2	3	4	5	6	7
I	ii	iii	IV	V	vi	vii°

Minor Scales:

1	2	3	4	5	6	7
i	ii°	-	iv	V	VI	vii°

3. We can use the **technical name** of the degree of the scale, plus major/minor/diminished as needed.

1	2	3	4	5	6	7
tonic	supertonic	mediant	sub-dominant	dominant	sub-mediant	leading note

The Roman numeral system is the most useful, because it lets us understand the triad in relation to the key of the music, and it's a nice, short way of writing triads. Make sure you learn the Roman numerals!

NAMING CHORDS

Triads are very "theoretical" things - we use them a lot when we analyse music, but we don't see them so often in practice. Triads only have 3 notes, but in real life, chords usually have more than 3 notes. Very often they have 4 notes, but can have many more.

The simplest kind of 4-note chord is a triad with the root repeated in a higher octave. (Sometimes the third or fifth of the triad is repeated instead of the root.)

The triad of C major: The chord of C major:

Chords which contain only the notes which **already** exist in the triad use the same naming systems as triads, so this is C major, or I (in the key of C major).

Another kind of 4-note chord is one which has a note **added** which doesn't exist in the triad, for example this one:

Here we've got a G major triad, with an F at the top. F is an interval of a 7th above the root, G, so we call this chord G7, or V7 (in C major). Or we can use the technical name of "dominant seventh" (in C major). Dominant seventh chords are extremely common. You've probably come across lots of them in your music making, but in fact for grade six music theory, you only need to be able to recognise them - you don't have to actually **write any**!

A2 TRIADS AND CHORDS EXERCISES

Exercise 1: Triad Quality

Identify the following triads as major, minor or diminished:

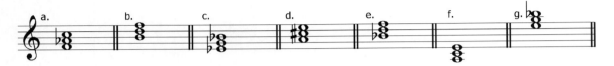

Exercise 2: Naming Triads

Name the following chords using the Roman numeral System (e.g. I, ii, iii etc).

Use capitals for major chords, lower case letters for minor chords, and lower case plus a small circle (°) for diminished chords.

Also give the key name of the chord (e.g. C major). The first one has been done as an example:

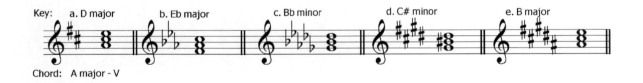

Exercise 3: Writing Triads

Add two notes to make the named triads, with the root in the bass. An example is given.

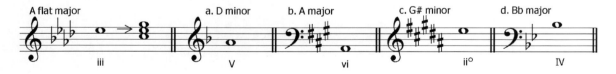

A2 TRIADS AND CHORDS ANSWERS

Exercise 1

   a. Minor
   b. Diminished
   c. Major
   d. Major
   e. Major
   f. Minor
   g. Diminished

Exercise 2

   b. F minor – ii
   c. Gb major – VI
   d. G# major – V
   e. A# dim – vii°
   f. Ab minor – ii
   g. B dim – ii°
   h. F# minor – i
   i. D minor – vi
   j. F minor – i

Exercise 3

A3 INVERSIONS
Look at the Bass Note

We know that triads are built using a root, 3rd and 5th. When we built triads in lesson A2 we always wrote the **root** as the lowest note (or **bass note**) of the chord.

However, we can choose another note of the triad to use as the bass note, without changing the basic nature of the triad.

We don't always use the root of the chord as the bass note when harmonizing music, because it tends to sound quite boring after a while.

When a chord's lowest note is **not** its root, we say the chord is **inverted** (like turned upside down). Let's look at inversions in more detail. We'll use the C major triad, to make things easier.

Root Position

The root of C major is C. When the root is the lowest note in the chord, we say the chord is in **root position.**

In the Roman numeral system, we write the letter "a" to show a chord is in root position. For example, "Ia" means a tonic chord with the root as the lowest note.

Root position chords are extremely common.

First Inversion

Let's change the order of the notes so that the lowest note, or "bass note" is an E. We are using the **third** of the triad, instead of the root.

In Roman numerals, we write "b" to show 1st inversion. "Ib" means a tonic chord with the third of the triad in the bass.

First inversion chords are quite common. Diminished chords are normally only used in first inversion.

Second Inversion

When we put the 5th of the triad as the bass note, we have a second inversion chord.

In Roman numerals, we write "c" to show 2nd inversion. "Ic" means a tonic chord with the 5th of the triad in the bass.

Second inversion chords are quite rare. We don't normally use 2nd inversions, except in special circumstances, for example, the "cadential 6/4" or "passing 6-4". These are explained in detail in the next lesson.

The Order of the Other Notes

When you're thinking about inversions, the only note you need to worry about is the **bass** note. It is the bass note, (or lowest note), which tells you which inversion a chord is in.

All the other notes of the chord can be written in **whatever order suits them best**.

So, for a c major chord in root position we could find any of these chords with a bass note C:

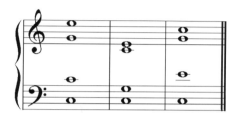

For C major in 1st inversion we could find any of these chords, which have a bass note E:

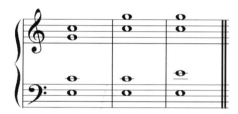

And for a C major chord in 2nd inversion, we could find any of these chords, which have a bass note G.

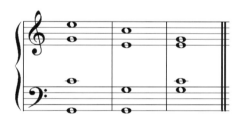

Third Inversion

Chords with an added 7th have another possible inversion: 3rd inversion, or "d".

Here's G7 (the dominant 7th in the key of C) in its four positions:

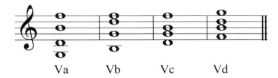

Va   Vb   Vc   Vd

You need to be able to **recognise** third inversion chords at grade 6, but you don't have to write any!

A3 INVERSIONS EXERCISES

EXERCISE 1: NAMING INVERSIONS

Name these chords using the Roman numeral, plus a letter (a, b or c) to show the inversion. The first one has been done as an example. The key is given.

Ia, IVc, Vib, vii°b, ii°b, Vc, ib, VIa

EXERCISE 2: COMPLETING CHORDS

Write one note **between** the given notes, to complete the following chords. The first one has been done as an example. The key is given.

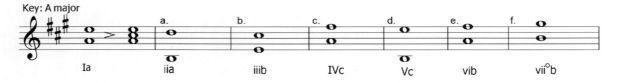

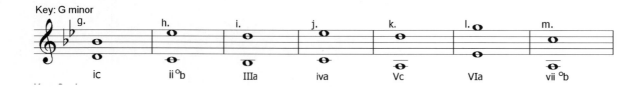

A3 INVERSIONS ANSWERS

Exercise 1

    a. IVc

    b. vib

    c. vii°b

    d. ii°b

    e. Vc

    f. ib

    g. VIa

Exercise 2

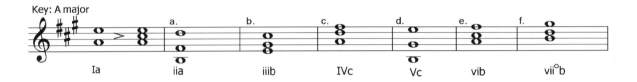

Key: A major — Ia, iia, iiib, IVc, Vc, vib, vii°b

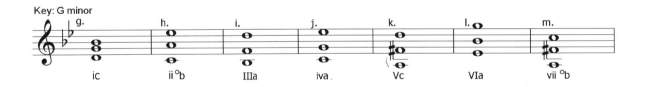

Key: G minor — ic, ii°b, IIIa, iva, Vc, VIa, vii°b

A4 CHORD PROGRESSIONS

What is Chord Progression?

The way we place chords next to each other is called "chord progression".

There is, of course, an infinite number of patterns of chord progressions, but there are also lots of "standard" patterns which our ears are very used to hearing.

Some chords sound extra-good when placed in certain progressions, so it's useful to learn what these progressions are.

We most often find "standard" progressions at the **end** of a phrase, or the **end** of a piece. Progressions at the end of a phrase or piece are called "cadences".

Standard progressions also happen at non-cadence points in music. One very common pattern is called the "progression of 5ths".

In this lesson you'll find an introduction to:

- Perfect, imperfect and plagal cadences
- The progression of fifths
- The passing six-four and the cadential six-four
- The V-VI progression

You'll also start to understand about **voice leading** - which means working out which voice (e.g. bass, tenor, alto or soprano) should sing/play which note of the chord (no, it's not totally random!)

Cadences

Cadences consist of two different chords, one after the other. Cadences which occur at the **end of a piece** of music are nearly always either V-I (called a "perfect cadence") or IV-I (called a "plagal cadence"). Of these two, the perfect cadence is much more common. In real life, you could see other progressions at the end of a piece. But in the Grade Six Music Theory Exam, you will **always** be expected to end a piece with one of these two cadences.

(A piece ends with a double bar line. Sometimes you might get a question which ends with a **single** barline - in that case it's not the actual end of the piece and so might not be a perfect or plagal cadence.)

Cadences which occur at the **end of a phrase** often, but not always, end on chord V (always major, even in a minor key). These are known as "imperfect" cadences.

Perfect Cadences

In perfect cadences, the bass line falls by a fifth (or rises by a fourth) and the chords are in **root** position. So, the perfect cadence is V**a** – I**a** (or ia in a minor key).

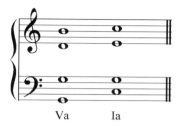

Va   Ia

Notice the voice leading (how each part moves separately) - see how:

- the bass root rises by a fourth (or falls by a fifth e.g. it could move to the C an octave lower here)
- the doubled root of V, (tenor G in this example), does not move - it becomes the 5th of I
- the 3rd of V, (soprano B in this example), **rises** to the tonic of I
- the 5th of V, (alto D in this example), **rises** to the 3rd of I

Plagal Cadences

In plagal cadences, the bass line falls by a fourth (or rises by a fifth) and the chords are usually in **root** position. The plagal cadence is IV**a** – I**a** (or iva-ia in a minor key).

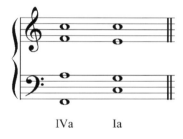

IVa   Ia

Notice the voice leading - see how:

- the bass root rises by a 5th (or falls by a 4th)
- the doubled root (alto part here) **falls** to the 3rd of I
- the 3rd of IV (tenor part here) **falls** to the 5th of I
- the 5th of IV (soprano part here) does not move and becomes the doubled tonic of I

Imperfect Cadences

At the end of a questioning phrase (not at the end of a piece) we often hear an "imperfect cadence". This is **any** progression which ends up on a dominant, chord **V**. The most common imperfect cadences are as follows (minor keys given in brackets):

- I-V (i-V)
- ii-V (ii°-V)
- IV-V (iv-V)
- vi-V (VI-V)

Chords I/i, ii/ii°, IV/iv, V and VI/vi can also be used in the first inversion.

As we'll see, ii/ii° leads us to V in the progression of 5ths.

Here are some examples of imperfect cadences:

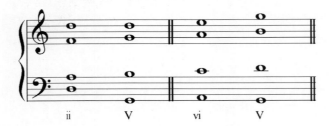

Notice the voice leading - see how:

- all chord notes except the bass move by the **smallest possible interval**.
- if a note occurs in both chords (e.g. D in the first example), keep it in the same part (soprano here).
- other notes move by semitone (half step), tone (whole step) or third. Don't use larger intervals.

THE PROGRESSION OF FIFTHS

As you know, lots of music ends with a V-I (or i) cadence. This is because the notes in chord V have a very strong "pull" towards those in chord I (or i).

For example, in the key of C major the chords V-I are G major - C major. The B in G major has a strong pull towards the tonic C. The semitone (half step) interval creates this strong pull.

Chord V is called the "dominant" for this reason - it's the most important chord after the tonic.

The 7th degree of the scale is called the "leading note" for the same reason - it feels like it **leads** somewhere, and the note it leads to is the tonic. We say that the leading note **resolves** to the tonic, because our ears feel satisfied when we hear the tonic played after the leading note.

So, chord I is most strongly related to chord **V,** its **fifth**.

In fact, every chord has a very strong connection with the chord which is a **fifth** higher. So, a chord of G has a strong link with the chord of D. In C major, D is chord ii (minor, not major), but that's ok - the link is still strong whether it's a major or a minor chord.

So far we have discovered that the following chords have a dominant-tonic relationship: I-V-ii

We can carry on in the same way, until we've used up all the triads of C major:

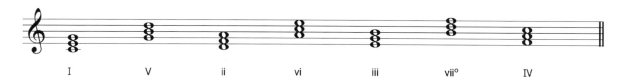

We now have the complete cycle of the **progression of fifths**. All we need to do now is reverse the order, so that each "dominant" chord resolves to its "tonic":

Progression of Fifths: I - IV - vii° - iii - vi - ii - V - I

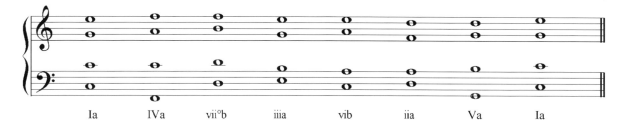

You will almost never see the **whole** series of fifths in use in one go. Usually just 2 or 3 chords are taken from it at one time, for example, you might see vi - ii - V, or ii - V - I.

The Cadential 6-4

Often, the perfect cadence is stretched over **three** chords, in what's known as a "cadential 6-4". "6-4" is another way of saying "2nd inversion chord".

The cadential 6-4 progression uses the chords **Ic** - Va (ic –Va in minor keys).

This is one of the very few occasions when you are allowed to use a second inversion (c) chord. (The inversions are very important here).

The bass note in chords Ic and Va is the **same** (in C major, for example, the bass note will be G in both chords).

The effect is that the bass **stands still** for a moment, while the chord above it changes. This "powers up" the bass note - our ears are expecting something important to happen - and when we finally hear the root position tonic chord Ia, with the bass dropping solidly by a 5th (or rising by a 4th), our ears (and brains) feel satisfied.

Here is a cadential 6-4 - pay particular attention to the bass line: two dominant notes (F#) are followed by the tonic (B).

Tip! Always see if you can use a cadential 6-4 at the end of a piece in your grade six exam. They are not always possible, but **if** they work, they are great!

ic   Va   ia

To use a cadential 6-4 correctly, you must be careful that

- the tonic of the Ic chord (e.g. B here) moves to the 3rd of the Va chord (A# here)
- the 3rd of the Ic chord (D here) moves to the 5th of the Va chord (C#)
- the 5th (bass note) of the Ic chord (F#) becomes the tonic of the Va chord, i.e. the bass line keeps the same note in Ic-Va. The octave can change (as here), or stay the same.

The Passing 6-4

The passing 6-4 is another progression where you are allowed to use a second inversion (6-4) chord. Unlike the cadential 6-4 where the bass note stays the same, in a passing 6-4 the bass moves **by step**. The second inversion chord falls on a **weak** beat of the bar.

Look at this passing 6-4 and notice that

Ia   Vc   Ib

- the bass line moves by step: C – D – E
- the second inversion chord (Vc) falls on a weak (middle) beat
- the other parts move by the smallest possible steps

V-VI Progression

Finally, we'll take a look at a progression which is very common in minor keys. The V-VI progression is a little bit special, because you have to **break** one of the general rules of harmony in order to use it!

The most important rule in harmony is that you don't write consecutive perfect fifths or octaves. You must **never** write consecutives. A "consecutive 5th" is when the interval between two parts is a perfect 5th (e.g. the bass and tenor have C & G) and the **next interval** (between the same two parts) is also a perfect fifth (e.g. the bass and tenor move to D & A). (See chapter A6 for more about consecutives).

Another rule of harmony is that you should avoid **doubling the major third in root position** chords. For example, if your chord is C major in root position, you shouldn't double the E. (The third can be doubled in first inversion chords, and minor root position chords).

However, in a minor key, when V moves to VI, you **have to double the third** in chord VI, in order to avoid writing consecutives. This is the only situation when you should double the third in a major root position chord.

Here's an example - the key is A minor.

Va   VIa

V is E major, so there is a fifth between the E and B of the chord. Chord VI is F major, with a fifth between F and C.

In Va-VIa, the bass E has to move to bass F.

G# is the leading note, so it moves to A.

The B would logically move to a C, because it's a semitone step (half step), but that would make a consecutive 5th with the bass, so we move it to A instead.

The soprano E again would normally move by step to F, but that would make a consecutive octave with the bass, so it has to move to C instead.

These are the only legal moves, and the end result is a chord of F with two As - which is a major third above the root F.

Don't worry if all this sounds a bit too confusing for now! The important thing to remember is that there are some progressions which require special treatment. Keep that in the back of your mind, and when you start doing harmonisations and find yourself getting stuck, come back to this page and see if it makes a bit more sense!

A4 CHORD PROGRESSIONS EXERCISES

Exercise 1: Cadences

1. Where do we normally find cadences?

2. How can you be sure that you are looking at the **end** of a piece, in the grade 6 exam?

3. Using Roman numerals, name the chords in a) a perfect cadence, and b) a plagal cadence.

4. Which chord does an imperfect cadence finish on?

5. Identify the following cadences as "perfect", "plagal" or "imperfect".

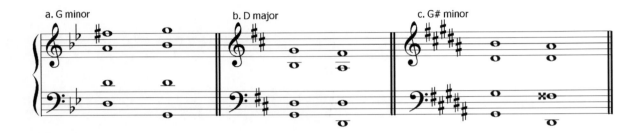

6. Complete the missing alto and tenor parts in these cadences. Keep the top two parts as close together as possible, and double the root of the chord. All chords are root position.

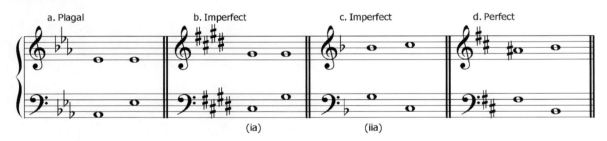

Exercise 2: Progressions

1. Complete the progression of fifths (major key): IV – vii° –

2. Which chords make up a cadential 6-4 (in Roman numerals with inversions)?

3. How does the bass line move in a passing 6-4?

4. Which two chords are a common progression in minor keys, where you have to "break" a rule in the second chord?

5. And which rule do you need to "break"?

6. Identify the second inversion chord in each extract, and then say whether it is part of a passing 6-4 or a cadential 6-4.

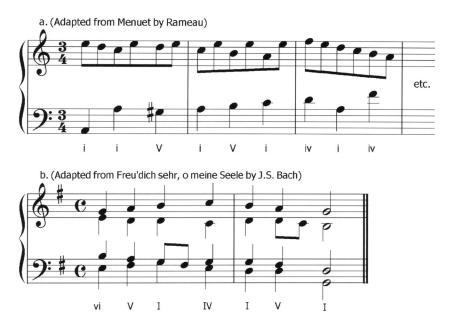

7. Write the chord notes to complete the following 6-4 progressions. Make sure each voice moves as little as possible, keeping the same note in the same part whenever you can.

A4 CHORD PROGRESSION ANSWERS

Exercise 1: Cadences

1. At the end of a phrase and the end of a piece.

2. There will be a double bar line.

3. a) perfect cadence V-I . b) plagal cadence IV-I

4. V

5. a) Perfect. b) Plagal. c) imperfect

6.

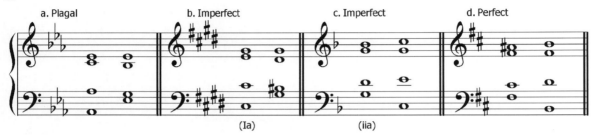

Exercise 2: Progressions

1 IV – vii – iii – vi – ii – V – I

2. Ic – Va

3. The bass line moves by step.

4. V – VI

5. You need to double the third in the major root position chord VI

6.

a) Passing 6-4

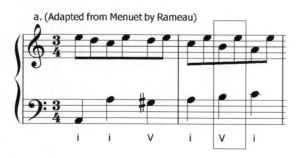

b) Cadential 6-4

7.

A5 MELODIC DECORATION

What is Melodic Decoration?

There are several ways that we can make a harmonic line more interesting - liven it up a little - so that it doesn't sound like a boring, simple progression of chords.

The different techniques we can use to do this are, as a group, called "melodic decoration", and can be found in any of the voices – Soprano, Alto, Tenor or Bass. Notes which form part of the melodic decoration are also sometimes known as "non-chord" notes, because they are not part of the actual chord chosen for the harmony.

Look at these bars taken from a Bach Chorale BWV 2.6. The first score shows the "bare bones" harmony - with one chord per beat.

Bach added some melodic decoration to this harmonisation, making it a lot more interesting. Can you spot all the differences?

Each type of melodic decoration has a name. You'll need to learn the names and how to recognise the decorations in a piece of music. For grade 6, you don't have to actually **write** any melodic decorations. But, you **will** see them, both in the harmonisation questions and in the general knowledge section (questions 4 & 5).

Types of Melodic Decoration

These are the types of melodic decoration or ("non-chord notes") you need to know about for Grade six theory:

Passing notes (accented, unaccented, chromatic & harmonic)	Changing notes	Suspensions	Pedals (tonic & dominant)
Auxiliary notes (upper, lower, accented, unaccented, chromatic & harmonic)	Anticipations	Retardations	

1. Passing Notes

A **diatonic passing note** falls in between two different notes which are a third apart. For example, the soprano notes C and E (figure 1) are a third apart. The D (marked *) falls between them, so it is a **passing note**.

Diatonic passing notes are notes that naturally occur in the key of the piece, like in the previous example. They happen when the two chord notes are a third (major or minor) apart.

Chromatic passing notes have an accidental added because they don't occur naturally in the key of the piece. For example, this passing note (figure 2) is C# - it falls between the two chord notes C and D. Chromatic passing notes occur between two note which are a major 2nd (or tone) apart.

These passing notes (figures 1 and 2) are **unaccented**, because they fall on an off-beat (between two chords).

Passing notes which fall on the beat are called **accented** passing notes.

Compare the following (figure 3) with the first example - this time the D is sounded on the beat - at the same time as the second chord. This time it's an **accented** passing note. An accented passing note forms a dissonance ("clash") with the rest of the chord, because the passing note is foreign to the chord.

FIGURE 1

FIGURE 2

FIGURE 3

2. Auxiliary Notes (also called "Neighbour Notes")

An auxiliary note falls between two **identical** chord notes. It can be higher or lower than the chord note. An auxiliary note which is higher than the chord note is an "upper auxiliary note" and a "lower auxiliary note" is lower than the chord note.

Auxiliary notes can be either **accented** or **unaccented**, just like passing notes. Auxiliary notes which are outside of the current key are **chromatic** auxiliary notes.

Here is an unaccented upper auxiliary note:

3. Changing Notes (Cambiata & Échappée)

There are two types of changing note.

The **cambiata** type is found **between** two notes which are often a fourth apart:

Look at the soprano line. The notes G-D are a fourth apart, and the changing note, F, falls between them. It's not a passing note, because passing notes always move by step.

The cambiata moves **down by step** (from G-F), then **falls by a third in the same direction** (F-D). The next note (E) is then a **step upwards** (D-E). This kind of decoration was more common in Renaissance music (1400-1600).

Try to learn it as **down 2nd, down 3rd, up 2nd**.

The échappée type of changing note falls **outside** of (i.e. not between) the two chord notes:

Look at the soprano line. B and G are chord notes. The C is the changing note.

The échappée moves **by step in one direction** (B-C) and then **by a leap in the opposite direction** (C-G), or vice-versa.

Try to learn it as **step one way, leap the other**. This kind of decoration was more common in Baroque music (1600-1750).

In the exam, both types are normally referred to as simply "changing notes", rather than by their specific names.

4. Anticipations

An **anticipation** happens when we write one chord note **earlier** than the rest of the chord - in the beat **before** the rest of the chord sounds.

Here, the B is part of the G major chord. The G major chord is sounded on the 2nd beat, but the B is sounded earlier, on the half beat before, so it is an **anticipation**. Anticipations are usually approached by a **downwards** motion (e.g the C **falls** to B).

The B is not part of the C major chord, even though it is heard at the same time. For this reason, it is a non-chord note.

5. Suspensions

Suspensions are the opposite of anticipations.

A **suspension** happens when we write one chord note **later** than the rest of the chord - during the beat **after** the rest of the chord sounds.

In this example, the B doesn't sound immediately with the rest of the G major chord - instead, the C from the C major chord is held on for a little longer, and then falls to the B half a beat **after** the G major chord has sounded. The C is not part of the G major chord, so it is a non-chord note. The C is a **suspension**.

6. Retardations

Retardations are a type of suspension. In the example of a suspension above, the C resolved **downwards** to B. In a **retardation**, the non-chord note resolves **upwards**.

Here the A resolves **upwards** to B.

7. Pedals

A **pedal** is either the tonic or dominant note played in one part continuously, while the chords in the other voices change.

Pedals normally occur in the bass, (but it is possible to find them in any of the other voices too).
The **pedal** note is either held on for a long time, or repeated several times.

Pedals which are not in the bass part are called "**inverted**" pedals.

Here's a tonic pedal (repeated tonic C):

And here's a dominant pedal (sustained dominant G):

NON-CHORD NOTES IN ACTION

Let's look again at the Bach extract at the top of this page, and try to work out some of the melodic decorations he used.

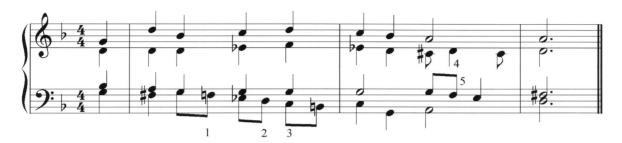

	Note	Type	Reason
1.	F	Unaccented passing note	F natural is part of the scale of G minor (melodic), so it's diatonic (not chromatic). It falls on the off-beat, so it's **unaccented**. It falls between two different chord notes, G and E flat, so it's a **passing note**.*
2.	D	Unaccented passing note	The passing note D falls between Eb and C, on an off-beat.
3.	C	Accented passing note.	This time the passing note falls on the beat, so it's an **accented passing note.**
4.	D	Upper auxiliary note	The D is between the two C sharps, so it's an upper **auxiliary** note.
5.	F	Unaccented passing note	It falls off the beat, so it's **unaccented**. It falls between two different notes a third apart, G and E, so it's a **passing note**. *

*Don't forget that the melodic minor version of the scale uses both E and E flat, and F natural and F sharp, because the note series is different on the way down.

33

A5 MELODIC DECORATION EXERCISES

A. Name the types of melodic decoration you might expect to see in the grade 6 exam: (the first letter has been given).

   a. A_____

   b. A_____

   c. R_____

   d. S_____

   e. P_____

   f. P_____

   g. C_____

B. Match these definitions to the types of melodic decoration from question A.

Definition	Type
a. "Down a 2nd, down a 3rd then up a 2nd" OR "a step one way, a leap the other"...	
b. They are notes which belong to the **previous chord** and they resolve **upwards**...	
c. They fall in between two different chord notes which are a 3rd apart...	
d. They are chord notes from the **previous chord** which resolve **downwards**...	
e. They fall between two identical chord notes...	
f. They are a tonic or dominant note played continuously...	
g. They are chord notes which belong to the **next chord**...	

C. The boxed notes are types of melodic decoration. Name the type for each one.

Include a full description: [accented, unaccented, chromatic, upper, lower] as appropriate.

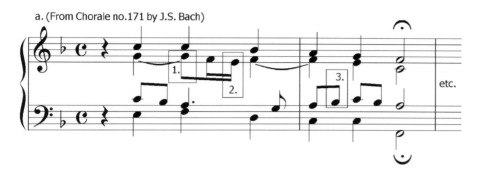

1.

2.

3.

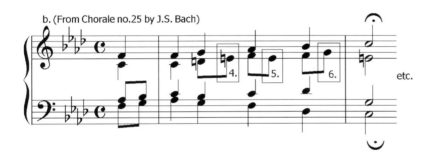

4.

5.

6.

7.

8.

A5 MELODIC DECORATION ANSWERS

A.

a. Anticipation
b. Auxiliary note
c. Retardation
d. Suspension
e. Passing note
f. Pedal
g. Changing note (or Cambiata)

B.

a. Changing note
b. Retardation
c. Passing note
d. Suspension
e. Auxiliary note (or neighbour note)
f. Pedal
g. Anticipation

C.

1. Suspension

2. Lower auxiliary (neighbour) note

3. Unaccented passing note

4. Unaccented passing note (the E natural is diatonic, not chromatic, because it is in the harmonic minor scale)

5. Lower auxiliary (neighbour) note

6. Changing note (échappée)

7. Accented passing note

8. Anticipation

A6 HARMONISING A MELODY I

In the grade 6 music theory exam, you have an optional question to harmonize a melody using Roman numeral notation (e.g. Va). (If you don't choose this question, you will need to do the question on creating a bass line using figured bass).

The question will look something like this:

Write chords at each place marked * to harmonize this melody.

Using Roman numerals, you need to suggest a chord **and its inversion** for each starred note. For example, you need to write "Va" for a root position dominant chord, not just "V". The starred note in the melody **must** be part of the chord you use to harmonise it, (or, occasionally, a recognised form of melodic decoration).

There are **many rules** which you need to try to learn. In this lesson, we will explain how to tackle this question, and what those rules are.

1. AVAILABLE CHORDS

In any key (major or minor), chords I, IV and V are the **primary chords** and II, III, and VI are **secondary**. Chord VII is so similar to chord V7 that it is not normally considered to be a chord in its own right, but a "V substitute".

Primary chords are essential for fixing the key of a piece. Chords I and V do this job together. Chord IV is not so important in this respect. For this reason, melodies should **always** begin and with I and V. It is possible (but not recommended) to harmonise every single note of the melody using only the primary chords. Your melody should also end with a **cadence** formed from primary chords. Chord V is major in a minor key (e.g. E major in the key of A minor).

Secondary chords are essential for creating an interesting harmony. This is especially true in major keys, where the primary chords are all major. You will need to make sure that some secondary chords are used in your harmonisation.

Chord III is rarely used. It is possible (but not recommended) to use it in a major key (where it is a minor chord, e.g. E minor in the key of C major). It is NOT possible to use an augmented III in a minor key, (e.g. C-E-G# in the key of A minor), but sometimes a major chord III is possible (because it's the relative major chord).

This leaves us with the following chords. (Capitals=major, lower case=minor, °=diminished)

Major keys: I – ii – IV – V – vi – vii°   Minor keys: i – ii° – iv – V – VI – vii°

2. Available Inversions

Major and minor chords can be used freely in **root position** (root note in the bass) or **first inversion** (third of the triad in the bass). You should use a good **mixture** of root position and first inversion chords.

Second inversion chords (fifth of the triad in the bass) can only be used in a passing 6-4 or cadential 6-4. (See lesson A3).

Diminished chords (vii° in all keys and ii° in minor keys) can only be used in **first inversion**.

Cadences should be harmonised with **root position chords**. Cadences which occur in the middle of the piece are more flexible, but aim to use the root position chords if you can. Cadences which occur at the end of the piece should only use root position chords.

Root position chords are notated with a lower case "a", first inversions are "b", and second inversions are "c". So, "Ic" means a tonic chord in second inversion.

Vb is only available if the leading note is **not** in the melody. You **cannot** double the leading note.

Never use Va-vib. The bass notes of these two chords are the dominant and tonic. Our ears expect to hear chord I with the tonic bass note after V, so the vi chord sounds wrong. For example, in C major, the bass moves from G to C. Play it on the piano!

Ia IVa Va vib

3. Repeating Chords

Change the chord with each starred melody note. Don't use the same chord twice (or more) in a row.

You can use the same chord in a different **inversion**, but **only when moving from a strong to a weak beat**.

For example, this harmonisation is ok, because chord Ib falls on a strong beat, and Ia on a weak beat:

But in this example, chord Ib falls on a weak beat (2nd) and Ia falls on a strong beat (3rd), so it's not ok:

Ib Ia Va

IVa Ib Ia Va

4. Consecutives

Consecutive perfect fifths and octaves are forbidden.

Check the interval made between the bass note and melody note. If it is a perfect fifth, you cannot follow it with another perfect fifth. The same goes for perfect octaves.

Va   Ia   IVa   Ib

The following bar shows a poor choice of chords. The first chord (Va) creates an interval of a perfect 5th with the melody, and so does the next chord (Ia). These are consecutive fifths. The third chord (IVa) creates a perfect octave with the melody, and so does the Ib chord which follows it. These are consecutive octaves.

Notice that here the intervals are actually **compound** fifths and octaves (i.e. more than an octave apart). This makes no difference: consecutive octaves and fifths are forbidden whether one or both of the intervals are compound or not. Diminished fifths do not cause consecutives when they are next to a perfect fifth, but you should avoid moving from a diminished 5th to a perfect 5th.

5. Augmented Melodic Intervals

Augmented melodic intervals are forbidden.

Vb   iib

Your bass line is automatically created when you choose the inversions of your chords. Check the notes in the bass line and make sure there are no augmented intervals. (An augmented interval is one semitone (half step) wider than a perfect or major interval.)

This choice of chords is poor. The bass line moves by an augmented 4th:

6. Cadences

Cadences are musical versions of punctuation. They signify a natural pause in the music. A comma is like an **imperfect** cadence – one which leads to chord V. We pause, but we are aware that more is going to come. A full stop (period) is like a **perfect** cadence (V-I). We are assured that an end has been reached.

Unlike in the grade 5 exam, cadences will not be pointed out to you. You need to work out where they are yourself. Cadences occur at the end of a phrase. You can usually spot them because there is

- A longer note value than elsewhere in the melody
- A pause mark
- A double bar line
- A combination of these

Aim to use root position chords at a cadence. Don't assume that the melody will end with a perfect cadence – sometimes you are given an incomplete melody, which might end with an imperfect cadence. Plagal cadences (IV-I) are also possible, but they are not used as much as the perfect and imperfect cadences.

7. Common Progressions

Lesson A4 discusses the common progressions in detail.

Aim to use the **most likely** chords in every case. The most typical progressions are:

Major Keys

- vi – ii – V
- ii – V – I
- Ic – Va – Ia
- V – vi
- IV – I

Minor Keys

- VI – ii° – V
- ii° – V – i
- ic – Va – ia
- V – VI
- iv – i

In each of these progressions, with the exception of V-VI, the **root** (but not necessarily the bass) rises or falls by a **fifth or fourth.**

Here is an example.

The chords are via – iib – Va – Ia. The bass line falls by a third from E to C, rises a second to D, then falls a fifth to G. The fundamental bass is given below the stave. This shows the **roots** of each chord. Each root rises or falls a fifth or fourth.

You are not restricted to root movement of fourths and fifths, but this kind of movement creates the strongest, most stable bass line.

You can also move the root by step (V-VI is an example, or IV-V).

Root movement by a third is weak, because the two adjacent chords share two common notes. For example, if F major moves to A minor, both chords share the notes C and A. You can use root movement by a third, but use it very sparingly.

Chord I can be followed by any other chord.

8. Contrary Motion

Whenever possible, aim to have the melody and bass line move in contrary motion (opposite directions) from each other. It won't always be possible, but it should be your first choice.

HOW TO TACKLE THE HARMONIZATION QUESTION

1. Work out the key (is it major or minor?)
2. Make a list of your available chords. Highlight the diminished chord(s), so that you remember to use them in first inversion.
3. Find the cadences. Complete these first, with root position chords. Use a Ic-Va-Ia progression if you can. Chord iib is often a good choice before Ic.
4. Harmonise the first two (or possibly three) chords with I and V, to establish the key.
5. Harmonise the rest of the melody, using a good mix of primary and secondary chords and mixed inversions. Use common progressions where possible. Write in the bass line as you go along, and with each note you write, make the following checks with the previous chord:
   - No consecutive perfect 5ths or octaves
   - No augmented melodic intervals
   - Chords are not repeated exactly
   - Repeated chords with different inversions fall on strong-weak beats

When you are working out your answer, it is **essential** that you write in the notes of the bass line, as you go along. This is the only safe way to make sure that your harmony is "grammatically correct".

Write in the Roman numerals only when you have decided on your chords, then erase the bass line notes, so that you are left with the Roman numerals only. This is the way your exam paper should be handed in for marking.

A7 HARMONISING A MELODY II

In this lesson we will walk you through a complete harmonisation. We will use the method outlined at the end of the last lesson. Here it is again:

1. Key?
2. List available chords for reference.
3. Harmonise cadences.
4. Harmonise start.
5. Harmonise the rest. CHECK everything.

Here is the melody we are going to harmonise. We've numbered the chords for reference.

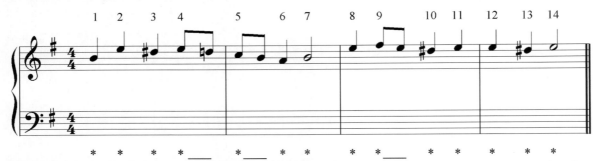

1. Key. The D#'s are a clue that the key is E minor. Also, the final note is E, and the beginning fits the chords of I and V in E minor.

2. Available chords:

I: E – G – B
ii°: F# - A – C [diminished!]
iv: A – C – E

V: B – D# – F#
VI: C – E – G
vii°: D# – F# – A [diminished!]

3. Cadences. There are two minims (half notes), which are a longer note value than used elsewhere in the melody, and therefore likely to mark cadences. The cadences are balanced with one at the half-way mark, and the other at the end. (Cadences can also be marked with a pause symbol, or double bar line). We will use root position chords, which make stronger cadences.

The first cadence is on A and B. These note fit an imperfect cadence. The B fits with chord V, but the A could fit with ii or iv, so we will leave this blank for now.

The second cadence is on the notes D# and E. These notes fit with V and i in E minor. Note 12 also fits with chord ic, which means we can use a cadential 6-4.

4. **Start**. We need to use chords i and V to establish the key of E minor. Note 1 (B), fits with both chords i and V. Note two fits with chord i, and note 3 fits with chord V. We could use V – i – V or i – i – V. Both of them are fine.

I'm going to use i – i – V. The first i falls on a strong beat, so it's fine to repeat the chord on the weak beat, as long as the inversion is changed.

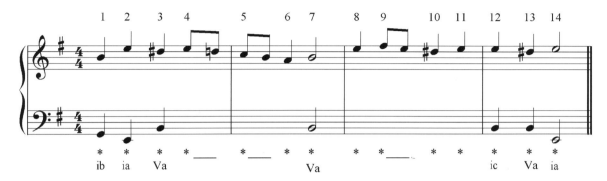

In chord 3, only Va is possible. Vb has a bass note of D#, which would cause consecutive octaves with the melody line.

Vc is not available, because the second inversion chord can only be used in a cadential or passing 6-4. It's not a cadence, and in a passing 6-4 the second inversion has to fall on a **weak** beat. Beat 3 is a strong beat (in quadruple time), so it won't work here.

5. **The rest**.

Chord 4 needs to contain an E. The D natural is a passing note and we can ignore it.

E occurs in i, iv and VI. We will choose chord i, because the root movement of a fifth will create a strong first bar. We could use i in root position or first inversion.

Since we've used ia more recently, ib provides more interest.

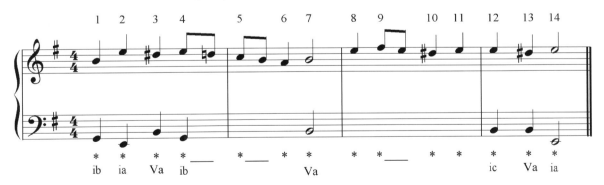

Chord 5 fits with ii°, iv or VI. Since there are lots of options, let's move on to chord 6, because it may be more restricted.

Chord 6 fits with ii°, iv and vii°. We can discount vii° for chord 6, because it is a "substitute V". Chord 6 falls on a weak beat, so it should be a completely different chord to chord 7. We can also discount chord ii°. The F# diminished chord has to be used in first inversion, which means the bass note must be A. This will cause consecutive octaves with the melody. Chord iva also causes consecutive octaves, so ivb is the only option here.

Back to chord 5.

Using ii or vi will produce a root movement by thirds, which is weak. If ii moves to iv, the two chords share the notes A and C. If VI moves to iv, they share C and E.

Although these chords are not illegal, I'd prefer to use iva. This chord movement also mirrors bar 1, which is nice.

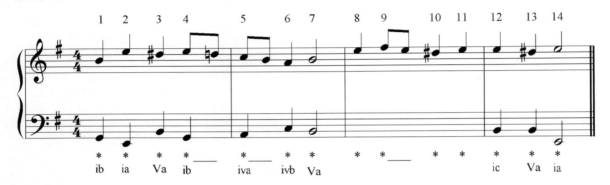

Chord 8 fits with i, iv and VI.

Chord ia is not available, because it will cause consecutive octaves (B-E). Chord ib is ok.

Chords iva and ivb are ok.

VIa is ok, but VIb causes consecutives again.

I will choose the root movement of a 5th for the strongest progression, so chord 8 will be ib.

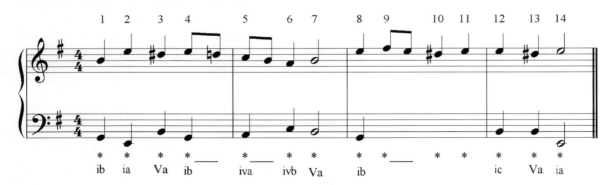

Chord 9 fits with ii°, V and vii°. Again, there are plenty of options, so we will come back to this one.

Chord 10 can only be V or vii°.

Since vii° is a V substitute, these are basically the same chord. We should, then, pick chord ii° for chord 9, so that the harmony changes. If we chose V or vii° for chord 9, the harmony would be repeated on a strong beat, which is poor.

Chord 9 has to be ii°b (because all diminished chords have to be in first inversion).

Chord 10 can only be Va and not Vb. This is because the leading note is in the melody (D#). You cannot double the leading note (i.e. it cannot be in the melody AND the bass at the same time).

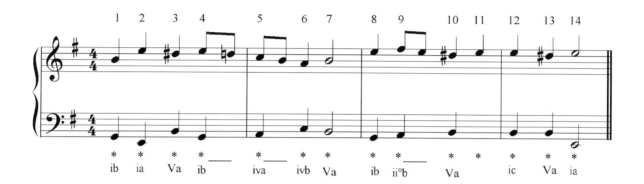

Finally we are left with chord 11. E fits with i, iv and VI.

Chord i is a bad choice, because we already have chord ic on the next strong beat.

V rarely moves to iv, but frequently moves to VI. This is one of the progressions listed in the "common progressions" in the last lesson. We can use VI here.

VIa will make the smoothest bass line, moving by step rather than a leap up to E in VIb.

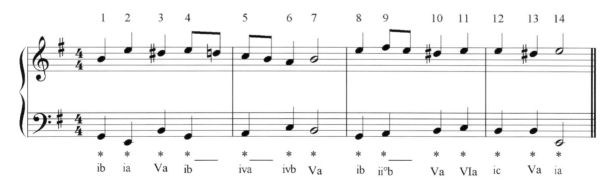

Don't forget to erase your working out when you've finished, leaving only the Roman numerals and inversions in place.

A6 & A7 HARMONISING A MELODY EXERCISES

For each melody below:

a) Name the key

b) Write out the available triads for each degree of the scale, and label them with the Roman numeral (e.g. I (C-E-G))

c) Harmonise the melody, using standard cadences and other common progressions where possible. Write out the chord using Roman numerals, including the inversion. Use a good variety of chords and inversions. Write out the bass line too, to help you check for consecutives.

Melody 1

a) Key:

b) Chords in this key:

Melody 2

a. Key:

b. Chords in this key:

Harmonising a Melody - Free Practice

The best way to improve your harmony is to practise as much as you can. Here's an activity you can try which will also improve your ability to "hear" music in your head. Start off with short phrases and try longer ones as you get better.

a) Think of a well-known children's song.

b) Sing it through in your head and try to work out which note is the tonic and what time signature it's in.

c) Grab some manuscript paper and try to write out the melody.

d) Play it through on your instrument, to check you got it right. (Correct any mistakes!)

e) Decide which notes need harmony chords, and which notes are passing notes (usually one chord per crotchet (quarter note) or minim (half note) is enough, but experiment). Mark the notes you're going to harmonize with a *.

f) Harmonise the melody.

g) Play it through on a keyboard **slowly** and really listen to what you've written.

h) Harmonise the same melody in a different way. (Try changing minor to major (or vice versa) as well!)

Here are some well-known British children's songs to get you started:
- My Grandfather's Clock
- Twinkle, Twinkle, Little Star
- Mary had a Little Lamb
- Sing a Song of Sixpence
- Ding, Dong, Bell
- Girls and Boys Come Out to Play
- Happy Birthday to You
- Sing a Rainbow
- Lavender's Blue
- I Had a Little Nut Tree

A6 & A7 HARMONIZING A MELODY ANSWERS

There are several different possible answers. Only one model answer is given here for each melody.

Melody 1

a. Key: C minor

b. Chords in this key: i (C-Eb-G), ii° (D-F-Ab), iv (F-Ab-C), V (G-Bnat-D), VI (Ab-C-Eb), vii° (Bnat-D-F)

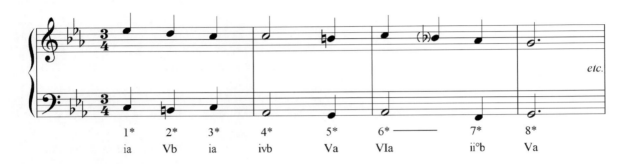

c. Start at the end, with the cadence. This is an unfinished piece, so we could use an imperfect cadence.

Chord 8: Va (choose root position at a cadence)

Chord 7: Almost any chord can lead to V in an imperfect cadence, but **ii°-V** is particularly good because the roots fall by a 5th (D to G). In a minor key melody, ii° is a diminished chord (D-F-Ab), so it can only be used in first inversion.

Now move on to the beginning, which should be harmonised with i and V to fix the key properly.

Chord 1: Ia – Tonic chord to establish the key.

Chord 2: Vb – To establish the key. Va would be ok as well.

Chord 3: ia – Be careful not to write B natural to Ab, which is an augmented interval.

Chord 4: ivb – The melody has a repeated C, so make sure the bass moves (don't repeat the previous note). Chord iv is a new chord so far – make sure you use a good variety of chords and inversions (a and b).

Chord 5: B natural only harmonises with Va (Vb isn't allowed, because you can't double the leading note) or vii°b. vii°b is no good, because Ab can't move to D natural - it's an augmented 4th.

Chord 6: VIa – The progression V-VI in a minor key is very common. VI is also a chord we haven't used yet, and it also continues the progression of fifths with the next two chords VI-ii°-V.

MELODY 2

a. Key: D major

b. Chords in this key: I (D-F#-A), ii (E-G-B), IV (G-B-D), V (A-C#-E), vi (B-D-F#), vii° (C#-E-G)

c. Start with the cadences.

| 1*___ | 2* | 3* | 4*_____ | 5* | 6*___ | 7* | 8* | 9*_____ | 10* |
| Ia | IVa | Va | via | Vb | Ia | iia | Ia | Va | Ia |

Chord 10: Ia - This is the end of the melody (notice the double bar lines) so it should end on the tonic chord. Use root position chords in final cadences.

Chord 9: Va - E and C# are harmony notes, so we will need a perfect cadence (V-I).

The minim (half note) half way through is a clue that there is a second cadence here. A midway cadence is likely to be imperfect, if the end cadence is perfect.

Chord 5: Vb (imperfect cadence).

Chord 4: via - The melody notes D and F# need to be harmonised. This gives us the option of vi (B minor) or I. We used vi because the secondary chord will make the harmony more interesting than using another tonic chord.

If we use via-Va we will create consecutive 5ths in the bass part (B in the bass and F# in the melody move to A in the bass with E in the melody). This isn't allowed. We chose via-Vb because it creates the smoothest (stepwise) bass line continuing from chords 1 and 2.

Now harmonise the beginning with I and V.

Chord 1: Ia – Tonic chord.

Chord 2: Iva - This can't be harmonised with I or V, so we picked the third primary chord – IV – instead. There are several possibilities here.

Chord 3: Va – We haven't used V yet, so it's important to do so at the first opportunity.

Chord 6: Ia – V can be followed by I or vi.

Chord 7: iia – We haven't used ii yet.

Chord 8: Ia – Ia-Va is a stronger progression than vib-Va.

A8 INTRODUCTION TO FIGURED BASS

WHAT IS FIGURED BASS?

Figured bass might look a bit mysterious if you've never seen it before. Even if you **have** heard of it, you might think it's rather strange!

So, let's find out what figured bass is all about.

This is what it looks like - the figured bass is the little numbers and accidentals written underneath the lower stave:

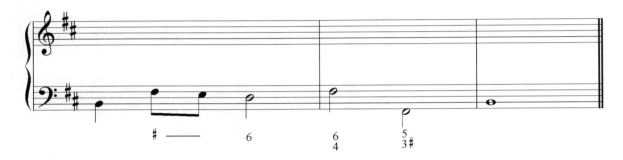

Figured bass is a shorthand method of composing. It was invented during the Baroque period (about 1600-1750). In those days, composers only wrote out a **melody** and a **bass line** (and not any of the middle parts). The melody was played (or sung) by a soloist, and the bass line was usually played on a keyboard instrument, such as the harpsichord or organ.

Obviously, the keyboard player needed to do a bit more than just play the bass line with his or her left hand, but where was the rest of the music? Well, he or she had to improvise!

The composer added small numbers underneath the bass line, like a kind of code, which told the player which chords to play. However, this code (which is the "figured bass") didn't tell the player **exactly** how to play the chords - for example, they could choose to play them as solid chords, broken chords or could weave them into heavily decorated individual voice lines.

In the modern world, you can find a similar kind of thing in sheet music for pop songs. Have you ever seen a tune written out with chord markings for piano or guitar? The accompanist uses the suggested chords, but plays them in whatever way they feel like. Figured bass is just the same, except that there are a few rules you have to obey - the rules of harmony.

Figured bass is hardly ever used today except in music theory exams, or in early music groups. So why is it tested? Well, it's been part of the study of music theory for hundreds of years and it's an excellent way to test your knowledge of harmony. Although no one composes using figured bass any more, it's still a useful way of referring to chords and chord progressions quickly. Figured bass is a compulsory part of Grade Six Theory.

Understanding Figured Bass

The Figures

Figured bass is written underneath the bass line. (Sometimes a bass line with figures is called a "continuo".) The numbers in figured bass tell you **what chord** to build up from the bass note, and in which **inversion.**

The single most important thing to remember about figured bass is that the bass line shows you the **lowest note**, and that you must build a chord **upwards** from that note. Never, ever write a chord note which is lower than the given bass note.

Each number tells you the **interval above the bass note** which you need to write, in order to create a chord. We will write all our chords as **4-note chords**, creating 4 independent voices – soprano, alto, tenor and bass.

(Note, although figured bass is really all about playing and improvising, rather than writing, we will talk about **writing** here because we are training you for an exam, after all!)

In Grade 6, there are three figures which you need to know; we call them "5-3", "6-3" and "6-4", pronounced "five-three" and so on.

Talking about Chords and Triads

Many students get confused about what is the "root", "bass", "third", "three" and so on in chords and triads. It is essential to have a clear understanding of how the parts of chords and triads are named, before continuing!

Triads: Triads are chords in their simplest, closest pattern. Triads contain three different notes, and each is a third apart.

The C major triad contains the notes C-E-G, **in that order**, for example.

In any triad, the first note is the **root**. The next note is the **third** (because it's a third higher than the root), and the last note is the **fifth** (a fifth higher than the root). All triads contain a root, third and fifth.

Chords: We are studying 4-part harmony, so all our chords will have four notes in them. The four notes are referred to by **voice**. Starting from the bottom, the four voices are **bass, tenor, alto** and **soprano**.

Each voice can theoretically sing any note from the triad. Therefore, the **bass** voice can sing the **third** of the triad, or the **alto** voice can sing the **root** of the triad, and so on. Chords are very flexible!

Chords usually contain the three triad notes plus one of them doubled, for example C-E-G-C (doubled root), G-E-C-G (doubled fifth) or E-C-G-E (doubled third).

Chords can also sometimes contain other combinations of notes from the triad, for example C-C-E-C (root tripled, fifth omitted).

INVERSIONS

The inversion of a chord is decided by the **bass** part note only.

- Bass note=root of triad> the chord is in root position.
- Bass note=third of triad> the chord is in first inversion.
- Bass note=fifth of triad> the chords is in second inversion.

5-3 CHORDS

5-3 means root position chord.

Look at the bass note (B). Add a note which is a fifth higher (F#) and another which is a third higher (D). This makes a root position chord: B-D-F#.

The F# and D can occur in any octave, and because this is four-part harmony, one of the notes will need to be **repeated**.

In this example chord, the B (root) is repeated in the tenor part, and the F# and D are on the treble stave, built as compound intervals (more than an octave) from the bass note.

The bass = the **root** of the triad

The tenor = the **root** of the triad (doubled bass note)

The alto = the **fifth** of the triad AND the **five** of the figure

The soprano = the **third** of the triad AND the **three** of the figure

Here is another example of the same figure interpreted in a different way. This time the root B is doubled in the soprano part, and the F# and D occur in the middle parts, the alto and tenor.

Because root position chords are so common, the "5-3" figuring is usually left out. If you see a bass note without any numbers at all, it means it's a 5-3 or root position chord. (It does **not** mean that you can write any chord you want!)

In a 5-3 chord, you can double the bass or 5th of the triad. The 3rd may be doubled in a minor chord, but it's usually better not to double the third at all.

6-3 Chords

A 6-3 chord is a **first inversion** chord.

The notes we need to write are a third and a sixth above the bass note.

Here is a bass note C. We need to add a note a sixth higher (A) and another a third higher than the bass (E). This gives us the chord notes C-A-E, with C in the bass. It is an A minor chord in first inversion, with a doubled root.

This is one way to write out the full chord:

Bass = **third** of triad (A-C-E)

Tenor = **root** of triad (A-C-E), or **six** of the figure (a 6th above the bass)

Alto = **fifth** of triad (A-C-E), **three** of the figure (a third above the bass)

Soprano = **root** of triad or **six** of the figure

Here is a different interpretation of the same figured bass. This time the third of the triad has been doubled (A-C-E).

Because 6-3 chords are also very common, they are usually just written as a lone **6** instead of **6-3**. The figure 6 means first inversion.

In a 6-3 chord, you can double the root of the triad, the 5th or the 3rd. In most major/minor chords it will be better to double the root or 5th of the triad. However, in a diminished chord, you should double the 3rd (which is the same as the bass note).

6-4 Chords

A 6-4 chord is a **second inversion** chord.

The notes we need to write are a fourth and a sixth higher than the bass note.

Here the bass note is C. The figured bass tells us to add F (a fourth above C) and A (a sixth above C). The chord notes are C-F-A, which is F major in second inversion.

Bass = **fifth** of triad (F-A-<u>C</u>)

Tenor = **third** of triad (F-<u>A</u>-C) or **six** of the figure (a 6th above the bass)

Alto = **root** of triad (<u>F</u>-A-C) or **four** of the figure (a 4th above the bass)

Soprano = **fifth** of triad (doubled bass note)

Here is another interpretation of the same figured bass note.

6-4 chords are always figured in full - they are not missed out or abbreviated like the 5-3 and 6-3 figures.

In a 6-4 chord you must always double the 5th of the triad, (which is the same as the bass note).

Chromatic Alteration

Figured bass sometimes includes sharps, flats or naturals. The accidental is written next to the figure which it affects.

If the accidental is not next to a figure, but just appears on its own, then it always refers to the **3rd** above the bass.

For example:

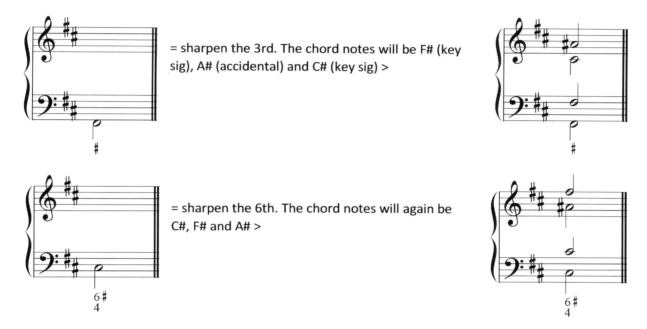

= sharpen the 3rd. The chord notes will be F# (key sig), A# (accidental) and C# (key sig) >

= sharpen the 6th. The chord notes will again be C#, F# and A# >

Chromatic alteration is very common in minor keys, where the dominant chord has a sharpened third which does not appear in the key signature. For example in A minor, the dominant chord is E major, with a G sharp accidental.

Lines

Horizontal lines in figured bass mean that the same harmony applies to two or more notes. It means "don't change the chord!"

A8 INTRODUCTION TO FIGURED BASS EXERCISES

Exercise 1

a. The figure 5-3 is used to show which position of chord?

b. The figure 6-3 shows which position?

c. The figure 6-4 shows which position?

d. What does a blank figure (with no numbers) mean?

e. What does a 6 on its own mean?

f. What does a short horizontal line mean?

g. A figured sharp sign on its own will affect which note of the chord?

Exercise 2

Add notes to make 4-part chords according to the figures on these bass notes. (There are several possible answers - make sure that you have doubled an allowed note, and that the gap between the tenor/alto and alto/soprano parts is not bigger than an octave).

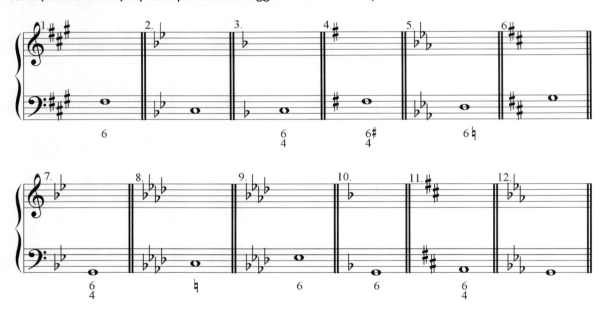

56

A8 INTRODUCTION TO FIGURED BASS ANSWERS

Exercise 1

a. Root position

b. First inversion

c. Second inversion

d. Root position chord

e. First inversion chord

f. Don't change the chord

g. The third above the bass

Exercise 2

There are many possible answers. Here are some suggestions:

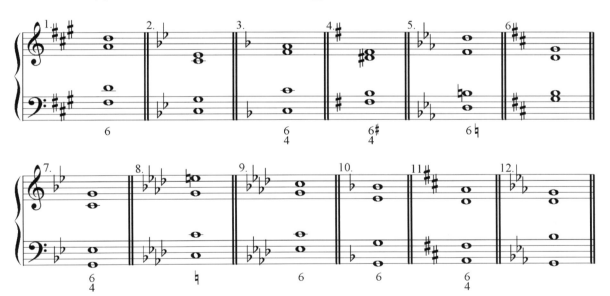

Comments:

In chords 3, 4 , 5, 7, 10 and 11, you **must** double the note that's in the bass part.

In chords 6 and 8, you **cannot** double the third of the triad.

A9 FIGURED BASS RULES

REALISING A FIGURED BASS

"Realising" a figured bass means "making it real" or, filling out the four-part harmony by adding a tenor, alto and soprano part.

Simply building up chords according the figures is **not** enough though, unfortunately! You need to abide by the rules of harmony as well, and aim to create a musical melody line (in the soprano voice).

In this section, we will exam the **rules** (unbreakable) and **guidelines** (break at your own risk!) which you need to memorise, in order to successfully realise a figured bass.

VOICE LEADING (RULES AND GUIDELINES)

"Voice leading" refers to the way each separate voice part is constructed, note after note. If you only build chords **vertically**, by simply looking at the figures, you will end up with a mess horizontally - each voice part will jump around in a crazy, unmusical way.

In this example, each individual chord has been correctly interpreted according to the figured bass, but the resulting individual voice parts are a terrible mess!

Play each voice part through separately, and compare how they sound with the bass line, which IS musical. Better still, try to actually **sing** these three upper parts - you are likely to find them quite awkward!

With good voice leading, each part will move **smoothly** to the next note.

- Soprano should move either by step or by a third (guideline)
- Alto and tenor should either repeat the previous note or move by step (guideline)
- Other intervals are allowed if you are stuck, but nothing bigger than a 5th (only the bass part can leap an octave) (guideline)
- No augmented or diminished intervals (if used there are rules about exactly how - best to avoid!)
- Parts should not cross (e.g. the alto part should not go higher than the soprano etc.) (rule)
- The leading note should always be followed by the tonic in the soprano part (rule)
- Don't write an interval of more than an octave between the soprano/alto parts or the alto/tenor parts (an interval of more than an octave is allowed between the tenor and bass parts) (rule)

In the previous example, the parts move by **unacceptable intervals** and the parts sometimes **cross**. The **leading note** (B) is not followed by the **tonic** (C), and the interval between the upper parts often **exceeds an octave**.

Here's the same bass with improved voice leading. Notice how much **easier** each part is to sing.

6   6   6   6

Consecutive Fifths and Octaves (Rule)

As mentioned in the "harmonising a melody" lesson (A7), consecutive perfect fifths and octaves are not allowed. In the "bad" realisation previously, the third and fourth chords in the soprano and alto parts contain consecutive octaves - G/G moves to A/A. This is not allowed.

The following are considered to be consecutives and are therefore not allowed:

a. perfect 5th followed by another, different perfect fifth in the same two parts

b. perfect octave followed by another, different perfect octave in the same two parts

c. compound intervals are also counted as consecutive e.g. F-C (perfect 5th) moves to G-D (compound perfect 5th) or vice versa

d. consecutives caused by melodic decoration notes, such as passing notes

e. consecutives **before** melodic decoration notes (the decoration cannot "fix" the consecutive)

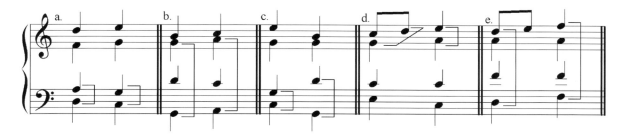

The following are **not** considered to be "consecutives":

a. perfect 5th followed by diminished 5th (acceptable)

b. diminished 5th followed by perfect 5th (not acceptable)

c. perfect interval followed by identical perfect interval e.g. C-C followed by C-C (acceptable)

Doubling and Omission (Rules and Guidelines)

When you are writing harmony in four parts you always need to double at least one note of the triad. There are rules covering each inversion, and you must also make sure that the choice of doubling creates the best voice leading, without creating consecutives.

- In a root position major chord, double the tonic as first choice. If the tonic is not available, double the fifth. Don't double the third (guideline, with the exception of the V-VI progression (see chapter A4)).

- In a root position minor chord, double the tonic as first choice, the fifth as second choice and the third as a last resort (guideline).

- In a first inversion major or minor chord, double the root as first choice, the fifth as second choice and the third as a last resort (guideline).

- In a first inversion diminished chord, double the bass (which is the third of the triad) (rule).

- In a second inversion chord, always double the bass (which is the fifth of the triad) (rule).

In addition, the following advice should be followed:

- Never double the leading note when it is followed by chord I (rule).

- Aim to use all three triad notes unless doing so breaks another rule (guideline).

- Only the fifth of the triad can be omitted - all chords need a root and third as a minimum (rule).

- If the fifth is omitted, either double the root and the third, or triple the root with a single third. Never triple the third (rule).

The Melody Line

Finally, here are some extra guidelines to help you write a good, musical melody line (soprano part).

- Move by step or by third as much as possible.

- Don't restrict the soprano part to a very narrow range of notes.

- Avoid repeated notes. A note repeated once is fine, but it's enough.

- Aim to make the soprano move in contrary motion (i.e. in the opposite direction to) the bass.

- If both the bass and soprano move by a leap (an interval wider than a 2nd), make sure they move in contrary motion.

- Don't write notes above A (one ledger line)

- Add some melodic decoration (passing notes or auxiliary notes) to liven things up. But watch out - notes of melodic decoration are also affected by the rules of consecutives. In fact, the chords must be free of consecutives both with AND without any melodic decoration (see consecutives, above).

A9 FIGURED BASS RULES EXERCISES

Exercise 1: Defining the Rules of Figured Bass

Choose the correct response(s) to complete the following sentences.

1. "Voice leading" refers to the way notes are put together vertically to make chords/horizontally to make melodies
2. In the soprano, the part should move mostly by an interval of a 2nd/4th/6th.
3. In the soprano, repeated notes should be avoided/used frequently.
4. In the soprano, the part should move in similar/contrary motion with the bass.
5. In the alto and tenor, the part should move frequently by unison/3rd/5th.
6. Augmented melodic intervals are encouraged/best avoided.
7. If, for example, the alto part rises higher than the soprano part, this is called oblique motion/crossing parts and it is allowed/not allowed.
8. Whenever possible, the leading note should be followed by the tonic/dominant/supertonic.
9. Consecutive 5ths occur when two parts are a perfect/augmented/diminished 5th apart and are then followed by another 5th using the same/different pitches.
10. Apart from consecutive 5ths, consecutives are also forbidden with perfect 4ths/perfect octaves/major thirds.
11. The interval between the soprano and alto parts should never be more than a 6th/7th/octave.
12. In a major 5-3 chord, the best note to double is normally the root/3rd/5th of the triad.
13. In a diminished 6-3 chord, the only note you can double is the root/3rd/5th of the triad.
14. In a 6-4 chord, the only note you can double is the root/3rd/5th of the triad.
15. In *almost* all cases, the most unsatisfactory note of the triad to double is the root/3rd/5th.
16. The mediant/subdominant/leading note should never be doubled.
17. The only note of the triad that can be omitted from a chord is the root/3rd/5th.
18. The only note of the triad that can be tripled in a chord is the root/3rd/5th.

Exercise 2: Spot the Errors

In each of the following bars, a **rule** of figured bass has been broken (not a guideline). Identify one error in each bar.

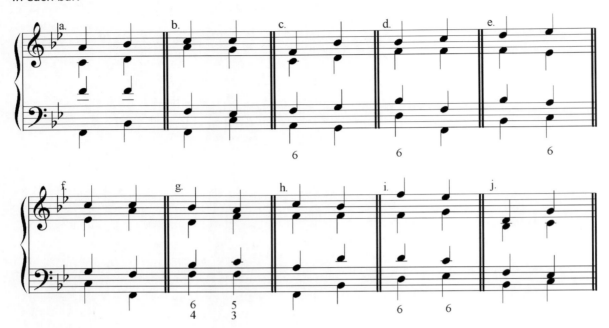

a.

b.

c.

d.

e.

f.

g.

h.

i.

j.

A9 FIGURED BASS RULES ANSWERS

Exercise 1

1. horizontally to make melodies
2. 2nd
3. avoided
4. contrary
5. unison
6. best avoided
7. crossing parts; not allowed
8. tonic
9. perfect; different
10. perfect octaves
11. octave
12. root
13. 3rd
14. 5th
15. 3rd
16. leading note
17. 5th
18. root

Exercise 2

[S=Soprano, A=Alto, T=Tenor and B=Bass]

a. Parts cross (A/T)

b. Alto and tenor are more than an octave apart

c. Consecutive 5ths (A/T)

d. Missing 3rd of triad in chord 2 (note A)

e. Incorrect doubling in chord 2 (double the bass because it's a diminished chord)

f. Augmented interval Eb-A in alto part (also, alto and tenor are more than an octave apart)

g. Incorrect doubling in chord 1 (double the bass, because it's a 6-4 chord)

h. Leading note must lead to tonic or dominant (A followed by Bb or F in tenor part)

i. Chord 1 is missing the root (Bb)

j. Consecutive octaves (A/B)

A10 FIGURED BASS REALISATION

These are the steps you need to follow in order to realise a figured bass line. A worked example is explained in this lesson. Details can be found in the previous two lessons.

The suggested method for working through a question is this:

1. Work out the key of the piece and make a note of which note is the leading note.
2. Write the whole soprano line.
3. Fill in the alto and tenor parts, chord by chord.
4. Check for errors and rewrite where necessary.
5. Repeat step 4.
6. Add melodic decoration if necessary

In addition, you will probably find it easier if you follow these guidelines:

- With every note you write down, check it with the previous note/chord for **consecutives** and **augmented/diminished melodic intervals**.
- With root position and first inversion chords (major and minor) always begin by trying to **double the root**. If you can't, try the fifth of the triad. If you can't, either double the third or omit the fifth.
- Pay close attention to all "6" chords - some of them may be diminished, which means you have to double the bass note (third of the triad).
- Try to sing through each individual voice part in your head. This is a quick way to identify augmented/diminished intervals.
- Only add melodic decoration if your soprano line is tedious. It is not necessary if the melody line is sufficiently interesting.

Here is the bass line we are going to realise. There are many possible ways to answer this question - this lesson will look at just one.

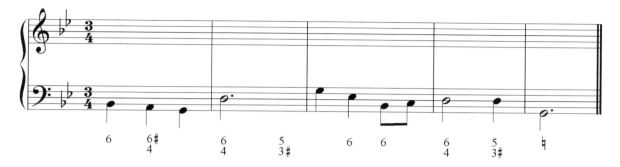

1. The accidental sharps in the figures, along with the final G, are clues that the key is G minor. This means the leading note is F# - be careful not to double this note.

2. Look at bar 1. The chords are G min (ib), D maj (Vc) and G min (ia). All of these chords contain a D, so D would be a poor choice for the melody to begin on (because we would end up repeating it in the next two or three chords!) Using contrary motion, we can make a mirror image of the bass line. Good soprano and bass lines often form mirror images, so aim to do it if you can.

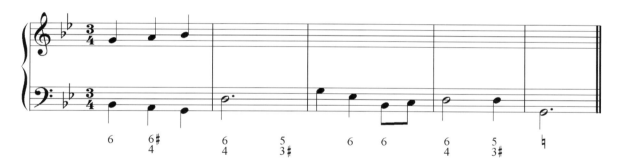

In bar 2, although there is only one bass note, there are two chords to realise - first a 6-4 chord (G min), followed by a 5-3 (D maj). Again, both chords contain a D, so we'll avoid putting that in the soprano part, to avoid repetition. We've already used Bb and A in bar 1, so using G and F# in the melody here will make the soprano line a bit more interesting.

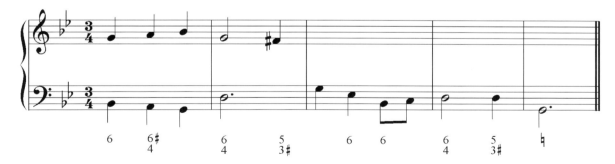

65

The leading note F# should be followed by the tonic G. After that, we could repeat the G (boring) or leap up to C. We can't fall to Eb, because it would create consecutive octaves with the bass. We'll follow the C with a Bb: again, we want to avoid those D's! Falling to G would make a rather bumpy melody line.

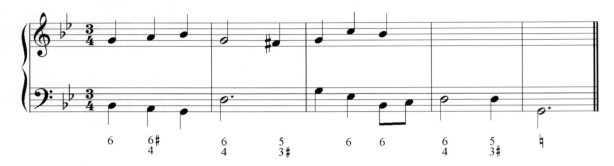

The last three chords form a cadential 6-4. We'll use Bb-A-B natural, because that allows us to write the alto part a third lower (G-F#-G) in close harmony. Don't forget to add the accidental natural to the last B!

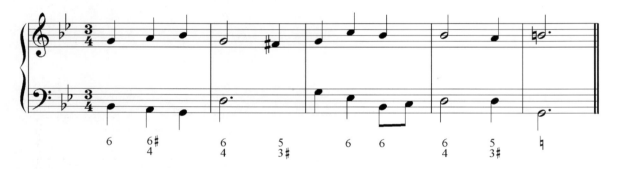

3. We now need to fill in the inner parts, checking each note as it goes down.

Place the alto and tenor notes of the first chord carefully. The soprano and alto should be relatively close together; the tenor and bass can be much wider apart. Double the root of the chord (as long as it is allowed!)

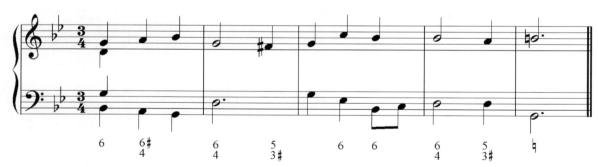

Continue each chord by writing in the **nearest possible allowed note**. Use repeated notes if you can, if not then move by step. Double the root whenever you can.

You can see that in bars 1-2 the alto part contains nothing but a repeated D. (Imagine if that was the soprano part!) The tenor part moves mostly by step. In the 6-4 chord the fifth is doubled (as per the rules), but in all the other chords it is the root which is doubled.

In bar 3, the alto leaps by a fourth to G - we could have used a step movement to Eb, but the resulting chord would be missing its fifth (G). We chose the leap, to achieve a fully sonorous C minor chord. In the last chord of bar 3, we doubled the third (Bb) in the melody line (see above), so we need the alto and the tenor to fill out the harmony with the root and fifth of the G minor chord.

Finally, the cadential 6-4 at the end is completed by using the smoothest voice leading possible. In any cadential 6-4, the voices must always move to the nearest note (or not at all!).

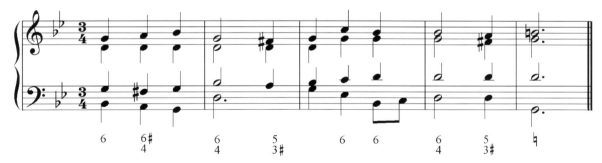

Again, the repeated D's belong to one part only - this time the tenor voice. The alto takes the third below the soprano, in close harmony. Apart from the 6-4 chord, yet again the **root is doubled** in each chord.

6. The soprano line is actually fine in itself - it's not too repetitive and uses enough different notes. However, we'll add some melodic decoration anyway! Look for places where the melody moves by a third (for passing notes) or has a repeated note (for auxiliary notes). Check very carefully that writing the melodic decoration does not introduce any illegal consecutives into your answer! We can add two non-chord notes: in bar 1 (passing note) and in bar 3 (auxiliary note):

Checking your answer is absolutely vital. It's essential to check as you go along, but you also need to double check everything when you've finished. Be systematic in your checking, or you will overlook something!

The Checks:

1. **Chord Notes.** Check that every chord contains the right chord notes and that the note you have doubled is allowed.
   Read each chord slowly and place a tick under it after it's checked.

2. **Consecutives.** Check each possible pairing of parts for consecutive octaves and fifths.
   Write out the following: S-A, S-T, S-B, A-T, A-B, T-B. Then follow each pair of parts, one at a time, checking the intervals carefully. Tick off each pair of parts as it's completed.

3. **Similar Disjunct Motion.** Recheck the bass and soprano lines together. If both parts leap, make sure that they move in contrary motion.
   Look along the soprano and bass lines, following the contours of the parts.

4. **Voice Leading.** Leading notes should resolve to the tonic in the soprano part, (in A/T they may also fall to the dominant), no illegal intervals, mostly stepwise movements.
   Read each part separately. If you see large intervals or anything suspect, double check that it's allowed. Sing through each part in your head.

5. **Cadences.** Cadential 6-4s must move in the proper way, 6 moves to 5, and 4 moves to 3.
   Look at the figures. If you see 6-4 followed by 5-3, it's a cadential 6-4. (If there is a 6-3 without the 5-3 after it, it's a passing 6-4 and more flexible).

6. **Overlap.** Make sure none of the parts overlap.
   Check particularly between the alto and tenor parts, as this is where errors creep in.

7. **Diminished Chords.** Diminished chords must have a doubled bass note.
   Look for first inversion ("6") chords and write out the letter names of the chord notes. If the chord is diminished, make sure the bass note is doubled elsewhere in the chord.

A10 FIGURED BASS REALISATION EXERCISES

Realise the following figured bass lines.

A10 FIGURED BASS REALISATION ANSWERS

The answers given are suggestions - there are many possible answers to these exercises. If you'd like MyMusicTheory to mark your figured bass exercises, email info@mymusictheory.com for more information.

A11 ADDING A FIGURED BASS LINE

In the grade six music theory exam, there are two questions which feature figured bass.

We previously looked at how to realise a figured bass, and earlier in this course we also looked at how to harmonise a melody. In this lesson we will look at the second figured bass questions: how to add a figured bass line, which is a combination of both! (This question is optional in the current grade 6 exams).

- **Realising a figured bass** means creating chords and melody from the given figures and bass line.

- **Harmonising a melody** means choosing chords to fit a given melody, and notating them with Roman numerals (e.g. Ib). You don't write out the bass line in the exam, but you need to work it out anyway!

- **Adding a figured bass line** means choosing chords and a bass line to fit a given melody, and notating them with **figured bass**. The bass line **must be written.**

To create a figured bass line, you need to follow these three steps:

1. **Choose chords** which progress without breaking any rules (consecutives, doubling, etc.) and which follow common progressions and cadences
2. **Write out the bass line** (i.e. the lowest note of each chord)
3. **Add figures** where appropriate, to show exactly which chord the player should build on each bass note.

Steps 1 & 2

The steps to choosing chords are the same as detailed in the two lessons on harmonising a melody. Re-read those units now if you need to refresh your memory. In a nutshell, the procedure is:

1. Using the melody, identify which chords fit each note and write them down.
2. Always start with chords I or V where possible.
3. Use root position chords in a cadence.
4. Use a variety of primary (I, IV, V) and secondary (II, VI, VII) chords elsewhere. Use a different chord on each harmonised note. Make the roots of each chord rise/fall by a 5th when possible (e.g. VI-II).
5. Pick each chord and inversion, **paying attention to the tune being produced in the bass.** Write the bass note and put the chord in **Roman numerals** for now. (We will delete the Roman numerals later).

You should:

- aim for contrary motion with the melody where possible, and always when both the melody and bass line move by an interval of more than a 2nd
- avoid augmented or diminished intervals in the bass melody
- avoid Va-vib or vice versa
- not write consecutive perfect 5ths or octaves
- make the bass line move mostly by a mix of intervals of 2nds, 3rds, 4ths or 5ths
- only write 2nd inversion (c) chords where there is a cadential or passing 6-4
- avoid doubled major thirds, especially when it is the leading note (e.g. D-F#-A in G major, F# is the leading note and shouldn't be doubled)
- avoid augmented chords (III+ in a minor key, e.g. C-E-G# in A minor)
- not anticipate the harmony on a weak beat (e.g. Ia – Ib with Ia on a weaker beat)

Step 3

Putting in the Figures.

You must follow the conventions for figured bass. The rules are:

a. Root position (5-3) chords should be left **blank** UNLESS they are part of a 6-4 progression (cadential 6-4), in which case write **5-3**.

b. First inversion chords (6-3) should be marked with just a **6**

c. Second inversion chords (6-4) should be marked **6-4**

d. In a minor key, you will often need to add accidentals to a chord, for example chord V should be major. In the figure, the accidental is written next to the number it affects, e.g. 6#. An accidental **without** a number refers to 3. For example, a # on its own is used as a short-hand way of writing 5-3#.

Here is a worked example. We are going to add a figured bass to this melody, assuming there is a change of chord with each star.

Notice that it starts on an A natural – this is an excellent clue that the piece is in D major, and not B minor. In B minor we would expect the leading note A to be raised to A#. We need to use chords I and V at the start, to fix the key properly.

We will add an imperfect cadence at the end. The last-but-one chord could be I or vi, so we'll note down both options for now.

Now to continue from bar 1. The note B fits with chord IV, which is a root fall of a fifth (D down to G), so therefore it makes a strong progression. I-ii is also ok. I-vi is a weaker progression because the roots move by a 3rd (D-B), which means the chords share two notes (D and F# in this case). I choose IV, because it is a primary chord with a strong root progression.

The note A fits with V and I (remember that iii isn't normally used). I choose chord V, because the progression I-IV-V is more varied than I-IV-I.

The note G fits with ii, IV and vii°. V-vii° is a root movement of a third (2 notes in common). V-IV is a root movement of a step (ok) and V-ii is a root movement of a 5th (strong), so I choose ii for this chord. In this bar, I can continue the progression of 5ths with ii-V-I. The second G in the bar can be treated as an **accented** passing note (between F# and A, but played on the beat). Most of the time melodic decoration will be unaccented, but always be aware that you **could** interpret some decoration as **accented** instead, which will open up more chord possibilities.

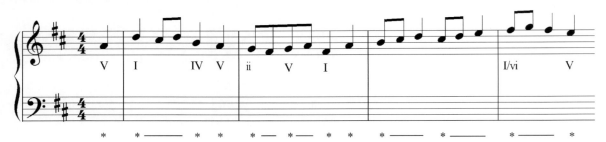

The note A fits with I, V and iii. We don't normally use iii, which means using a different inversion of I, or using V. I'll choose V.

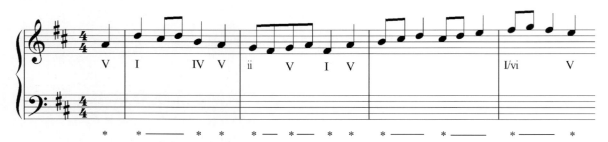

The next chord has to fit both B and D. The C# is a passing note. This gives us the option of IV or vi. I choose vi, because I haven't used it yet elsewhere.

Finally, the notes C# and E need to fit with the next chord. This gives us V or vii°. Both of these chords lead to I, so we will pencil in both of them, and change the next chord to a definite I.

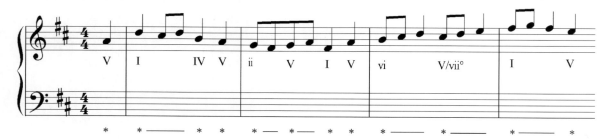

The next step is to work out which inversions are best. Remember:

- no consecutive 5ths and octaves with the melody
- no augmented or diminished intervals
- no second inversions except at a cadential or passing 6-4
- don't use Va-vib
- the leading note must lead to the tonic
- no leaps of a 7th

Start at the beginning and with each inversion you choose, check it with its neighbouring chords to make sure none of the above rules are broken. For example, you can't begin this piece with Va-Ia, because it would create consecutive octaves with the melody.

Write in ALL of the figured bass figures as you are working out your answer, including the 5-3 chords. This will help you to keep track of where you are. Erase all unnecessary figures when you have finished: all 5-3's except those in a cadential 6-4, the "3" of 6-3's. Make sure you have included any necessary accidentals (in minor keys). Here is a possible answer:

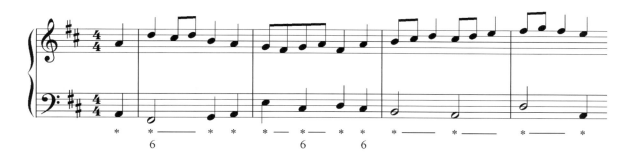

Notice that:

- the bass line tends to move either by step, or by 4th/5th
- the bass line does not go very high up on the stave
- the melody and bass line move in contrary motion most of the time
- there are no augmented or diminished melodic intervals in the bass line
- a variety of chords and inversions have been used

A11 ADDING A FIGURED BASS LINE EXERCISES

Add a bass line using figured bass at each place marked with a star. Root position chords should be left blank except when they are part of a 6-4 progression or chromatically altered.

a.

b.

c.

A11 ADDING A FIGURED BASS LINE ANSWERS

Suggested answers. Many correct answers are possible.

a.

b.

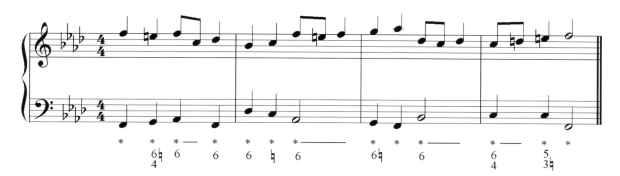

c.

B GRADE 6 COMPOSITION - INTRODUCTION

GRADE 6 COMPOSITION QUESTIONS

In the Grade Six music theory exam, composition is a compulsory question. It's worth 20% of the whole exam. You will have a choice of question. Both options will ask you to continue a given opening, and will be for instrument rather than voice.

One option will invite you to continue a "real life" opening (usually by a well-known composer from the Classical or Romantic eras) and the other will be an opening which has been specially written for the exam.

The "real life" opening usually needs to contain a specific key change. The melody should end in the new key. This is because the melody you write is really just the beginning of a bigger piece (which will never get written, however!) Although the name of the composer and work are given, you are not supposed to know how the piece goes and write the same notes as in the original! Even if you do know the opening, you need to write something new. The melody should be 8-10 (complete) bars in length.

For the "invented" opening, you are usually advised that a key change is optional. You may get a higher score if you write a good key change, so it's worth learning how to do it. In this question, the melody is complete in itself. This means that it shouldn't end in the new key – it should end in the same key that it started in. The melody should be at least 8 bars long.

WHAT THE EXAMINERS ARE LOOKING FOR

Never forget that this is a **music theory** exam, not a composition exam! Although you are writing a composition, you will be judged on your skill in applying the rules of accepted techniques, rather than displaying amazing creativity or innovation. Your composition should fit in with the norms which apply to music written from the 17th to 19th centuries.

The things the examiner will be looking for are the basis of this composition course. In a nutshell, they are:

- Form (good organisation)
- Harmonic structure (suitable expected chords to harmonise the melody)
- Melodic structure (showing continuity but with variety)
- Performance directions (relevant and appropriate)

The examiner is NOT looking for:

- Innovation (e.g. something new in every bar, new ways of getting sounds from an instrument, non-diatonic key systems)
- Proof that you know every ornament, tuplet, scale, broken chord, foreign term and symbol etc. that exists.

B1 ARCHITECTURE
How Compositions are Built

You wouldn't try to build a house from scratch without first looking at a lot of different types of building, and without reading up on the techniques of house construction. Similarly, it's a good idea to begin learning about composition by examining other people's work and studying the techniques they used.

If you compose without thinking about technique, you're unlikely to score a high mark in your Grade Six music theory exam!

We'll start by looking at the overall structure of a piece of music. The ABRSM book "Music Theory in Practice Grade Six" tells us that "music, unlike noise, is the result of **planned** use of sounds, ordered and controlled to make a logical progression".

This is really crucial – an unplanned composition will generally sound random and pointless and sometimes downright irritating!

We can compare music to language in many ways. If we think about language, the smallest units we have at our disposal are the individual letters of the alphabet.

We can arrange and group the letters to make words. We can't just stick any old letters together if we want our words to be meaningful! We arrange words into sentences, and sentences into paragraphs.

We could write out the possible progression like this:

Letter > Word > Clause > Sentence > Paragraph > Chapter > Book > Series etc.

In music, we start with a note. We combine small numbers of notes together to make a **motif**.

We might combine motifs in a couple of **sections**, which together make up a **phrase**. A couple of phrases will make a **sentence** and a bunch of sentences will make up a **section** (of a different type!) A handful of sections could comprise a **movement**, and three or four movements can make up a **piece**.

Note > Motif > Section > Phrase > Sentence > Section > Movement > Piece etc.

In the same way that language structure has some flexibility (not all books have chapters, for example), musical forms also vary a lot.

Some parts are indispensable however – there are no words without letters, and there are no motifs without notes.

Complete Piece or Complete Melody?

In the Grade Six music theory exam, you will have a choice of composition questions. You can either write:

- a melody which forms a **complete piece**, or
- one which is a **section of a larger piece**.

The composition techniques are more or less the same though, whichever option you choose. You will need to pay close attention to the wording of the question.

"Complete piece" means that the composition:

- **ends** at the last bar you write, and
- has to end on the tonic of the **original key**.

"Complete melody" means that

- we can assume the piece will **continue** with more music after what you've written, and
- it usually ends in **related key**, for example the dominant.

Structure

A typical eight-bar melody is divided up into two phrases, each of four bars.

The first phrase is the **antecedent** and the answering phrase is the **consequent**. Each phrase might be further subdivided into two two-bar sections.

Each section normally contains **connected motifs** or **melodic sequences** of notes. The similarity of these "musical words", and the harmony underlying them, is what gives the melody a feeling of coherence – it is not just a random series of notes.

It's important to remember that a phrase does not have to start on the first beat of the bar. But each phrase will contain the **same number of strong beats**.

EXAMPLES

Here are some examples of eight-bar melodies. Each eight-bar melody is made up of two complementary phrases.

Notice how, in each case, the melody is developed from the material in the first two bars by means of **simple changes**. The phrases are **similar** but **not the same**.

Our first example is from Mozart's Piano Sonata no. 3, K. 281.

- The antecedent phrase is from bars 1-4, and the consequent phrase is from bars 5-8.
- Each phrase is sub-divided into two sections (bars 1-2, 3-4, 5-6 and 7-8).
- The first section in both phrases begins with a dotted quaver (dotted 8th note) trill followed by two sextuplet groups (six notes in the time of four).
- The first section of the second phrase begins an octave lower than that of the first phrase, but is identical in every other way.
- The second section in each phrase contains some rhythmic material which is the same (the demisemiquaver (32nd note) rhythm) and some which is different.
- In bar 3, the harmony on the first beat of the bar is IV-I. In contrast, in bar 7 the chord is ii.
- Both phrases end with perfect cadences.
- The last three notes in bar 8 belong, in fact, to the next phrase. These are simply decorative linking notes.

Our second example is from a piece called "Rigaudon" by Handel.

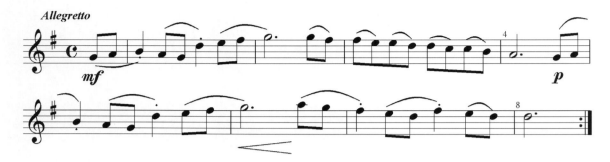

- The first section of the antecedent and consequent phrases is identical, except for the dynamics.

- The second section of the first phrase contains a quaver (8th note) sequence, whereas the second section of the second phrase re-uses the quaver-quaver-crotchet (8th-8th-quarter) rhythm from the first section.

- The first phrase ends with an imperfect cadence I-V.

- The second phrase ends with a modulation to the dominant – D major. This is a perfect cadence ending on the tonic D in the new key.

Our final example comes from a Waltz by Schubert. This melody is actually the second 8-bar section of the piece, and it leads on to another contrasting section.

- The first section of each phrase has the same rhythm, but the final minim (half note) is a different pitch, which means the harmony will also be different.

- The first section of the first phrase ends on the dominant of B minor (F# major) – the D on the last beat of bar 4 is an accented passing note and C# is the chord note. The first section of the second phrase ends on the dominant of D major (A major), which is the relative major key.

- Bar 7 re-uses the rhythm of bar 4, with a different melodic shape.

- The final three notes are decorative linking notes which belong to the next phrase.

- The modulation to the relative major key is helped by the A natural in bar 6. The harmonic B minor scale uses A#, but A natural is in D major.

B1 ARCHITECTURE EXERCISES

1a. The composition question in the Grade Six exam is optional – True or False?

1b. What percentage of the exam is the composition question worth?

1c. For each of the following i-iv, say whether it is usually a feature of composing

A - a complete **melody** OR
B - a complete **piece**

i. it ends in a new key

ii. it ends in the original key

iii. it is based on a real-life opening

iv. it is based on an opening invented for the exam by the ABRSM

2a. Draw slur marks over the antecedent and consequent phrases, and label them.

Old French Carol

2b. How is bar 3 similar to bar 2?

2c. What is the melodic material in bar 5 based on?

2d. What cadence do you think it ends on?

2e. Using only chords I, IV and V, choose one suitable chord for each bar.

Write the Roman numerals underneath the stave.

3a. Draw slur marks over the antecedent and consequent phrases, **and their sub-sections**, and label them.

3b. Describe the similarities between bars 1 and 2.

3c. Describe the similarities between bars 3 and 5.

3d. The melody in bars 5, 6 and 7 is based on triads. Name the chords which fit each group of notes marked A-D, using Roman numerals.

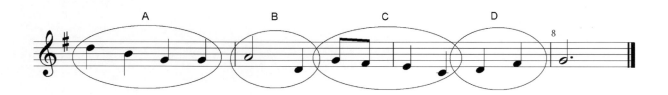

3e. What kind of cadence does it finish on?

B1 ARCHITECTURE ANSWERS

1a. False

1b. 20%

1c.

i. A

ii. B

iii. A

iv. B

2a.

2b. It is based on the same chord (I), it has the same rhythm, it has the same notes except that the C is an octave higher in bar 3.

2c. Bar 5 is based on bar 4. Both bars contain a fall followed by an upward movement by step.

2d. Perfect cadence.

2e.

(In bar 7, the E is an appoggiatura – chord V is necessary to make the perfect cadence.)

3a.

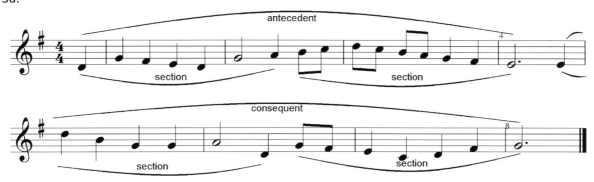

3b. Bars 1 and 2 both contain four notes which move by scale-step. Both bars start on G.

3c. The notes which fall on the beat are the same for beats 1-3 (D-B-G). (In bar 5, the C and A quavers (8th notes) are just passing notes, so essentially the melody is the same in beats 1-3).

3d. A=I, B=V, C=IV and D=V.   3e. Perfect cadence.

B2 MOTIFS & SEQUENCES

Motifs

A motif is a short, memorable unit of music.

Motifs which are as short as just one or two beats' worth of music can be glued together to make up a phrase. Typically, motifs are re-used throughout a piece to give a sense of continuity to the music. Although not all pieces of music contain motifs, most do, and they are a useful weapon to have in your arsenal of compositional techniques!

Arguably the most famous motif in classical music is the four-note sequence from Beethoven's Fifth Symphony:

The motif is repeated many times throughout the first movement. Sometimes the pitch is altered, sometimes it is sped up, but it keeps its character. The character of a motif is usually defined by its **rhythm**.

When you develop the opening material given in the Grade Six music theory exam, you will need to decide which element is interesting enough or promising enough to work as a motif. You then need to make sure the motif reappears in the rest of the piece enough times for it to become a "characteristic" of your composition.

Examples

Here are some examples of motifs in action. Play them through and notice how the motifs are altered in **simple ways** in order to give a feeling of continuity with variety.

Our first example comes from the Waltz in A flat by Brahms, Op.39 no.15. The motif is a dotted crotchet (dotted quarter note) followed by three quavers (8th notes), with the following "rough" melodic shape ("down-repeat-up"):

All the notes are taken from the chords which make up the underlying harmony, or in other words, they are all **chord notes**.

The melodic shape of the motif is pretty constant too – the first two notes are lower in pitch than the third, and are repeated, and the final note is the same pitch as the first (or close enough).

Here are the first eight bars. (Listen to the whole piece here at http://javanese.imslp.info/files/imglnks/usimg/5/5f/IMSLP74647-PMLP06507-waltz14.mp3 – you will notice the motif occurs throughout.)

The motif occurs 5 times here, and then a final time in the 8th bar as a linking sequence into the next phrase.

(Note – you only need to write a single line of melody for the Grade Six music theory exam, not chords.)

Our second example is from Rachmaninov's Prelude for Piano in G minor, Op.23 no.5.

The motif is a rhythmic unit: quaver – semiquaver – semiquaver – quaver (8th-16th-16th-8th). It is usually made up of the notes of the underlying chord. The first quaver (8th note) is stressed and forms part of the melody. The other three notes are repeated and are of a higher pitch and form part of the accompaniment.

Here are the first 5 and a bit bars. Listen to the whole piece at

http://pianosociety.com/cms/index.php?section=180.

Melodic Sequences

A melodic sequence is a series of notes which is repeated but with a **different starting note**. The basic **intervals** between consecutive notes are kept the same.

Usually all the notes are taken from the scale which forms the key of the piece, and therefore they aren't "chromatically altered" in any way. Sometimes however, chromatic alteration does take place. We'll take a look at both types of sequence.

Here's a simple melodic fragment of five notes:

The melodic interval between notes 1 and 2 is a second. Actually it's a **major** second, but we don't need to know the interval's quality (major/minor etc.) at the moment.

We can write out all the intervals between consecutive notes: 1-2=2nd; 2-3=3rd; 3-4=2nd; 4-5=3rd.

Next we will change the starting note – let's pick G. We then write out the melody again, based on those intervals, but still keeping to the notes available in F major:

This is a "diatonic" melodic sequence.

This means that the notes are chosen to **fit in with the scale**, rather than to be an exact match of intervals. Why so? When we examine the quality of the intervals, we'll see that they are different.

	Notes 1-2	Notes 2-3	Notes 3-4	Notes 4-5
Starting on F	Major 2nd	Minor 3rd	**Minor** 2nd	**Major** 3rd
Starting on G	Major 2nd	Minor 3rd	**Major** 2nd	**Minor** 3rd

The interval quality has changed from notes 3-5.

This gives the sequence a slightly different character to the original, but of course in many respects it is the same. This simple modification makes a new fragment of music which has both **continuity** with and **variety** from the original material.

What happens if we try to match up the intervals exactly? We get a "chromatic" sequence instead of a "diatonic" one.

We need to add in some accidentals in order to preserve the interval quality, and these accidentals will usually have the effect of making the music change key. This is also known as "modulation". Here's what happens when we match the intervals exactly.

The only change we needed to make was to raise the Bb up to a B natural. But because B natural doesn't occur in the scale of F major, we sense that the music is changing key. We feel as though G is the new tonic, and that therefore the music has modulated to G major.

Play these two 4-bar extracts, and notice how the first seems to stay firmly rooted in F major, but the second appears to modulate to G major:

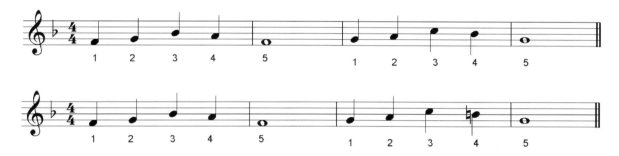

Hopefully by now you've got an impression of how useful melodic sequences are in composition. Sequences are hugely powerful devices when it comes to developing musical ideas. They allow you to easily write connected but contrasting fragments of music, and with a simple tweak here or there they can be used to make your music change key in the bat of an eye! You will notice that diatonic sequences are a lot more common than chromatic ones, as you would expect.

EXAMPLES

We will finish this lesson with an example of a diatonic and a chromatic sequence. Whenever you are playing any music at all, you should take a moment to stop and look carefully at what has been written, and see if you can spot any sequences in action. See if you can work out whether they are diatonic or not, and, if they are chromatic, what key do they lead to?

Our first example is from the opening of Mozart's Piano Sonata no.14 K457 in C minor. It is a diatonic sequence, played first from the tonic in bar 1 (C), and then from the dominant note (G) in bar 5. Other minor changes (marked by arrows in the extract) take place along the way.

Chromatic sequences are a lot less common than diatonic ones. However, you probably know this famous example, from the song "Do – Re – Mi" from the musical "The Sound of Music".

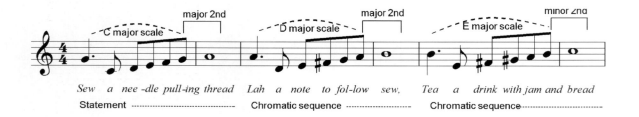

- The sequence consists of a 2-bar phrase.

- It starts with the first six notes of the C major scale, ending with a major 2nd.

- The next two bars form an exact chromatic sequence – the starting note is one tone higher and the six notes are from the scale of D major, with the F sharpened with an accidental.

- The third instance of the sequence is almost the same (up a tone, E major scale for the first five notes), but it ends with a minor 2nd interval.

B2 MOTIFS AND SEQUENCES EXERCISES

Exercise 1

Circle each further instance of the motif which was circled at the beginning of the score. Comment on any rhythmic modifications of the motif you find.

a.

b.

Exercise 2

For the following melodic sequences, say which key the music appears to be moving to.

a. (Starts in E major)

b. (Starts in G minor)

Exercise 3

Circle the notes in each of these given openings which would most likely make an interesting rhythmic motif to reuse elsewhere in the composition. The first one has been done as an example.

Exercise 4

In each melody, identify with a curved line a *statement* and one subsequent *melodic sequence* and label them as such. Say whether the sequences are **diatonic** or **chromatic**. The first one has been done for you as an example.

EXERCISE 5

Write the following melodic sequences as instructed, then sing or play them on your instrument.

a. Make two diatonic sequences of the opening. Start on the 7th degree of the scale to finish the first bar, and start on the 6th degree of the scale to complete the second bar. The key is B major.

b. Make two diatonic sequences of the opening. Start on the 2nd degree of the scale to complete bars 3-4, and start on the 3rd degree of the scale for bars 5-6. The key is Eb major.

c. Make a diatonic sequence of the opening in bars 3-4, starting on the 2nd degree of the scale. Make two more diatonic sequences to complete bars 5-6, using the first three notes of bar 5. Start the first one on the 7th degree of the scale and the second one on the 6th degree of the scale. (Use the melodic minor scale.) The key is F# minor.

B2 MOTIFS AND SEQUENCES ANSWERS

Exercise 1

a.

In the last motif, the middle two notes have been swapped around, so that a quaver is followed by a semiquaver (16th note).

b.

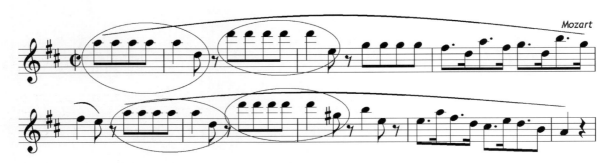

Exercise 2

a. The music is moving to B major, the dominant key.

b. The music is moving to Bb major, the relative major key.

EXERCISE 3

EXERCISE 4

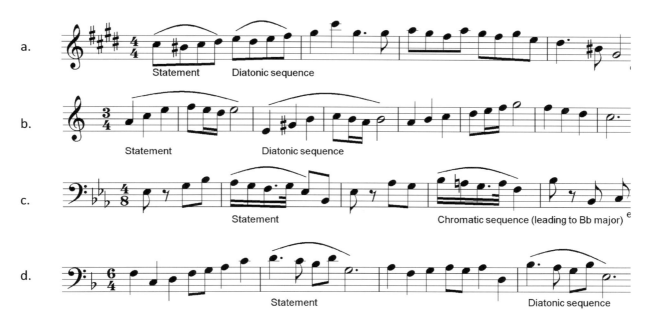

Exercise 5

a.

b.

c.

B3 CADENCES

QUICK REVISION OF CADENCES

If you took grade five music theory, you already know a lot about cadences. We will review them anyway, however! A cadence is a sequence of chords which concludes a musical phrase.

- The **perfect** cadence Va-Ia signifies a close. It's usually found at the end of a piece or main section.

- The **plagal** cadence IVa-Ia also has a final effect, but is softer and less dramatic.

- An **imperfect** cadence, e.g. ii-V or vi-V, is often found at the end of an antecedent (questioning) phrase, or at the end of a middle section of the music. (Any cadence which ends on V is an imperfect cadence.)

- An **interrupted** cadence, e.g. V-vi, is quite a rare type of cadence. Interrupted cadences are so named, because instead of following chord V with chord I as is usually expected, V is followed by vi (in a major key) or VI (in a minor key). Other variations are possible, but chord vi/VI is the most common.

- An **inverted** cadence, e.g. Vb-Ia, can also occasionally be found at the end of the antecedent phrase or the end of a middle section. An inverted cadence is one where a chord is in first inversion instead of in root position.

WHY DO CADENCES MATTER IN THE GRADE SIX MUSIC THEORY COMPOSITION?

Although you are going to compose an **unharmonised** piece in the grade six music theory exam, it's vital to realise that there should still be an **implied** harmonic structure to the melody.

This means that the notes you choose for the melody at the **half-way point** and at the **end** have to fit with the chords which would make up the cadences. If you choose notes which lie outside these chords, your cadences will not sound clear and you will lose points on structure.

Remember that "notes which fit" can include passing notes and other non-chord notes – you don't have to stick to the notes from the triad, but the triad-notes should be prominent. For example, if the implied chord is C major, you could write this, because the D and the F would be passing notes, leaving C-E-G as the triad.

But if you wrote this:

the implied chord would probably be D minor, although most of the actual notes are the same as in the first example. Why is this?

- Notes which fall on **strong beats** have prominence. In the second example, the F falls on the strong beat but is not part of a C major chord. (In duple and triple time, the strong beat is the first beat of the bar. In quadruple time there is a secondary strong beat half way through the bar.)

- Notes which fall **on the beat** have prominence. In the first example this is C-E-G. In the second it is F-G-D.

- Notes which are approached by a **leap** have prominence. In the second example, the D is approached by a larger interval than the other notes, but is not part of a C major chord.

- Notes which are **repeated** have prominence. The repetition of the F in the second example makes it stand out.

Your composition will most likely contain two cadences; an imperfect or interrupted cadence at the half-way point, and a perfect cadence at the end. If you choose the question in the Grade Six music theory exam which asks for a modulation at the end of the melody, your perfect cadence will be in the **new key**.

EXAMPLES

The following simple melodies illustrate how the notes chosen for the melody reflect the implied harmony. Our first example is from an Allegro moderato by Mozart (K.3 – written when he was six years old!)

- These twelve bars lead up to the end of the first section.

- The piece is in Bb major, and the first six bars of this extract are in Bb major, but the introduction of the E natural in bar 7 signifies that the music is modulating to F major – the dominant key.

- At the end of bar 5, the note A is a part of chord V in Bb major (F major), and the Bb in bar 6 is part of chord I.

- In bar 11, the G is a very prominent note because it falls on the strong beat and it is sounded three times. It is the dominant note of the dominant chord in F major (C major), and the section ends on a tonic F major chord in the new key.

- Both cadences are perfect.

Our next excerpt is from an Andante Grazioso in Bb by Haydn. (I have simplified it a little, to show just the melody.)

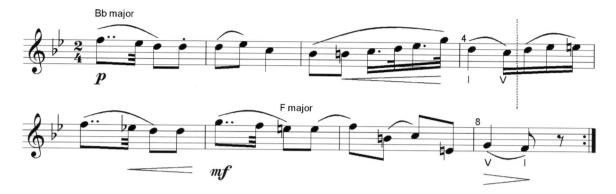

- The antecedent ends with an imperfect cadence in Bb (I-V).

- The last three notes in bar 4 are linking notes leading to the consequent phrase, and are not part of the cadence.

- The introduction of the E natural in bar 6 signals the beginning of a modulation to F major, the dominant key.

- The B natural in bar 7 does **not** signal a modulation to C major. Why not? Because the notes which fall on the beat in bars 7 and 8 are F-C-G-F – the Fs are prominent and the C and G are part of chord V in F.

- The phrase ends with a perfect cadence in F major, the new key (C-F).

Our final example is from a well-known Christmas carol, "It Came upon a Midnight Clear", set by Arthur Sullivan.

- There is no modulation from F major.

- The antecedent phrase ends with a chord IV followed by either a I or a V. This means it could be either a plagal or an imperfect cadence.

- The final cadence is perfect.

B3 CADENCES EXERCISES

Exercise 1

Give the name (e.g. "perfect", "plagal" etc.) of these cadences:

a. V-vi

b. I-V

c. Vb-i

d. vi-V

e. iv-i

f. V-I

g. ii-V

Exercise 2

Which chord is implied in each of these bars of melody? State the key (you are told whether it's major or minor), the chord in Roman numerals (e.g. V) and the letter name of the chord (e.g. C major). Name one chord only, per stave.

a.

b.

c.

d.

e.

Exercise 3

Each of the following melodies has a two-chord cadence, indicated by the brackets. State the chords implied in the bars as Roman numerals (e.g. V) and give the name of the cadence (e.g. "plagal"). (Each cadence contains two chords.)

a. (Eb major)

b. (Ab major)

c. (E major)

d. (Bb minor)

e. (A minor)

B3 CADENCES ANSWERS

Exercise 1

a. Interrupted

b. Imperfect

c. Inverted

d. Imperfect

e. Plagal

f. Perfect

g. Imperfect

Exercise 2

a. Key: D minor. Chord: i – D minor

b. Key: B major. Chord: IV – E major

c. Key: F minor. Chord: i – F minor

d. Key: D major. Chord: V – A major

e. Key: G minor. Chord: VI – Eb major

Exercise 3

a. V-I = Perfect cadence

b. ii-V = Imperfect cadence

c. V-vi = Interrupted cadence

d. iv-i = Plagal cadence

e. VI-V = Imperfect cadence

B4 INTERPOLATION

Although it's very common for musical phrases to be exactly balanced (e.g. four bars plus four bars), it's certainly not always the case.

A sophisticated technique, which involves a padding out of the second phrase, is called **interpolation**.

Instead of having two 2-bar sections in each phrase, the second phrase could contain three 2-bar sections, for example, resulting in a consequent which is six bars long:

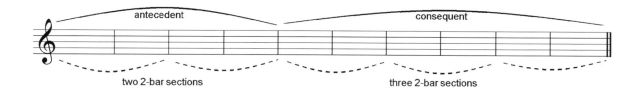

There are no hard and fast rules about interpolation sections – they can be different lengths and they are definitely not a compulsory part of the Grade Six music theory exam.

However, you may get more points if you can use interpolation **effectively**!

The instructions in the theory exam paper usually ask you to write a piece which is 8-10 bars in length, or at least eight bars long. A ten bar piece can be written with the structure 4+6, as shown above.

Interpolation is an effective technique because it is something which heightens our expectations and therefore increases the dramatic impact of the music.

Our brain "expects" (subconsciously) each phrase to be balanced, so when the final phrase is extended in this way we become more alert to the music, waiting for the end to materialise.

It creates a "wait for it!" moment. There is a feeling of tension or suspense, momentarily, which is only resolved when the final cadence is reached.

EXAMPLES

Our first example comes from Mozart's Piano Sonata no.1, 3rd movement.

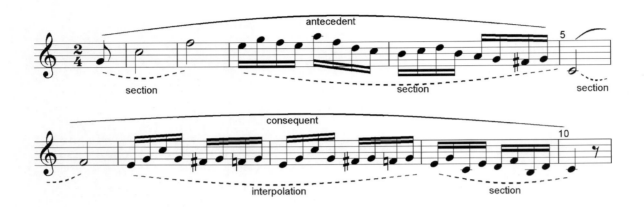

- The antecedent is four bars long, and the consequent is six bars long.

- Each phrase comprises two minims (half notes) followed by several semiquavers (16th notes).

- The interpolation section begins in bar 7, although the listener will not be aware that there is an interpolation until bar 8.

    We are expecting semiquavers (16ths), because we heard them in the antecedent phrase in bar 3, and that's what we get.

- In bar 8, we would normally expect the phrase to end.

    This means we anticipate longer note values, most likely a minim (half note) or crotchets (quarter notes), and also probably a perfect cadence.

    Instead, we hear the exact same semiquaver (16th note) segment from bar 7, repeated.

    The cadence is delayed, which adds tension and suspense.

- The perfect cadence and longer note values we expected by bar 8 appear in bars 9-10.

Our second example also comes from Mozart, and was chosen because it also illustrates that even antecedent phrases do not have to be balanced into two 2-bar sections. But notice that there still **is** balance and structure! This extract is 14 bars long – look at it carefully to see how 14 is achieved with balanced sections! This is Mozart's Allegro in F, K15a.

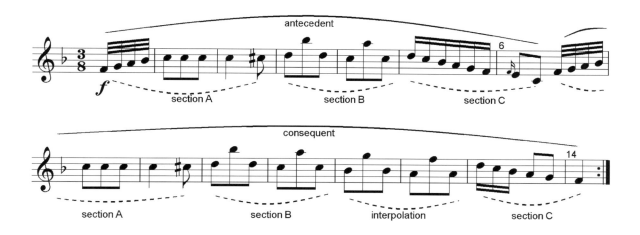

- The antecedent is 6 bars long, and the consequent is 8 bars long.
- The antecedent contains three 2-bar sections.

    (Remember that the length of a section or phrase is calculated by the number of **strong beats** it contains.)

- The consequent contains three 2-bar sections and a 2-bar interpolation.
- In bar 11 we are expecting something similar to bar 5/section C, but instead we hear the rhythmic motif from section B again, as a melodic sequence.

    The end of the phrase is delayed.

- In bar 13 we get the descending scale semiquaver (16th note) segment we were expecting in bar 11.

B4 INTERPOLATION EXERCISES
Exercise 1

1. Choose the right words to complete this paragraph.

Interpolation means shortening/extending the normal length of a phrase in a composition. Interpolation is used because it decreases/increases the tension towards the end/middle of a section.

2. Each of the following extracts has been taken from Mozart's Piano Sonatas. Each extract is ten bars long.
For each extract:
- draw phrase marks to indicate **one** antecedent and **one** consequent phrase
- if the extract contains an interpolation, mark its beginning and end
- there may be bars **after** the consequent phrase which belong to the following section – if so mark them as such.

a.

b.

c.

B4 INTERPOLATION ANSWERS

Exercise 1

Interpolation means **_extending_** the normal length of a phrase in a composition. Interpolation is used because it **_increases_** the tension towards the **_end_** of a section.

Exercise 2

a.

b.

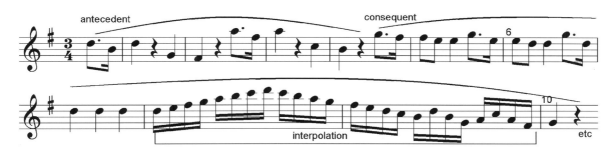

c.

B5 KEY AND TONALITY

WHAT IS TONALITY?

All music from the era we are studying at grade six (17th – 19th centuries) is **tonal** music. What does that mean?

- It has a key, which must be either major or minor. The key signature at the beginning of every line states the key of the piece as a whole.

- It may or may not move through other keys (modulate).

- The notes are mainly (but not only) taken from the scale of that key.

- In every key, the most important note is the tonic, and the next important note is the dominant.

- Every note in the scale can be harmonised by using one of only three chords – the tonic (I), dominant (V) or sub-dominant (IV). For this reason, they are known as the "primary" triads.

The aim is for a piece of music to have a clear, unambiguous key. With your music theory skills, you should be able to look at a score and quickly identify what key the piece is in, and whether it modulates to any new key(s).

You need to remember that the available chords are those built on each degree of the major or **harmonic** minor scales. This means that in a minor key, chord V is major (e.g. E major in the key of A minor) and chord vii° is diminished (G# dim in A minor). Chord III+ (augmented) is not available at all - you can't use C-E-G# in the key of A minor.

STATING THE KEY

The main key of a piece will be asserted at the beginning. In the Grade Six composition question this is especially important, because you will need to work out what key the music is in, in order to continue writing.

Using the key signature, we can easily narrow it down to either the major or minor of that particular key signature. But if we, for example, see a key signature of 1 sharp, how can we discover whether the music is in G major or E minor?

There are a few things we can try:

- Work out what the likely tonic is (G or E).

- Find a sharpened leading note (D#)

- Work out the likely primary chords (I, IV and V, or i, iv and V) (or V7) of the underlying harmony.

Which of these factors is the most important? It is the **harmony**, which is the most important factor in determining key.

1. Likely Tonic

The tonic is the most important note in a piece. It can be reinforced by:

- Occurring on a strong beat (first beat of the bar)
- Being accented
- Being repeated
- Occurring as the highest or lowest note of a phrase
- Being approached by a leap
- Occurring in part of a scale

2. Raised Leading Note

Seeing a leading note sharpened with an accidental can be a quick give-away that the music is in the minor key. However, bear in mind the following points:

- Not all melodies contain a leading note, so the piece might be in E minor but not contain a D# at all.
- In a descending minor scale passage, the melodic minor is often preferred, which means the leading note will not be raised.
- An accidental may be just a chromatic alteration because it sounds nice, rather than a signal of the minor key.

3. Primary Chords

The underlying harmony is the **most important factor** in determining key. The majority of pieces begin with chord I. A smaller number begin with V, but it's rare to find any other chord in this position.

Chord I is commonly followed by one of the other primary chords, so in the first couple of bars we would normally expect to find I, V and/or IV. Only chords I and V have the power to fix the key of the piece firmly in our mind. As the melody develops, any other chords can be used of course.

Let's now examine two simple "openings" and, by looking at the **underlying harmony**, try to determine whether it is the major or minor key in each case. Is this C major or A minor?

- Bar 1 fits with both i in A minor and I in C major. (The B is a passing note.)
- Bar 2 could fit with VI in A minor or IV in C major. (All the notes form the F major triad.)
- C major is a better choice, because it would use two primary chords – I & IV

This opening is identical, except for the last note:

- Bar 2 could be i in A minor or vi in C major.
- A minor is a better choice, using the tonic triad in both bars.

EXAMPLES

Is this G major or E minor? (The piece is "Rigaudon" by Rameau.)

- There are no sharpened leading notes to help us.
- The notes which fall on the strong beats are G and B – both of these notes are in the tonic triad of the major and minor chords, so that's no help.
- The lowest note of the segment is E, not G.
- There is a 6-note ascending scale of E minor. G major has only a 4-note stretch.
- E is repeated 4 times, G is heard twice.
- Bar 1 contains all the notes of the E minor triad, but not of the G major triad.
- In bar 1, the notes of the E minor triad fall **on** the beat G-E-G-B.
- Bar 2 could be harmonised with i in E minor or vi in G major, but chord vi isn't a primary chord.
- All the signs suggest that this is E minor.

Is this Haydn Minuetto in C major or A minor?

- There is a sharpened leading note G#. But, there is also a G natural, so we need to be careful.
- The notes which fall on the first beat of the bar are C and G#.
- A is the highest note and is also approached by a leap, which suggests A minor.
- C is repeated three times, A only twice.
- Bar 1 contains all the notes of the tonic triad in C major. This is chord III in A minor – not a primary chord, and not even a normal chord in A minor, which usually has a G# which makes an augmented triad (C-E-G#).
- Bar 2 is tricky, but could be harmonised with chord ii in C major, with the extra notes considered to be non-chord notes. In A minor it would be chord iv. This bar doesn't help us much.
- There are clues in these bars which point us in both directions. In cases like these, always give more importance to the **harmony** underlying the piece, rather than melodic clues. It is harmony which defines a key.
  Bar 2 would fit in with either key, so that leaves us with bar 1, which is clearly in C major, as the notes form a C major triad. Therefore, this piece is in C major.

B5 KEY AND TONALITY EXERCISES

Exercise 1

a. Which one of these indicators is the **most** important to consider, when we want to work out what key a piece is in?

   i. what instrument the piece was written for

   ii. whether the leading note is sharpened or not

   iii. what the first note of the piece is

   iv. what chords would fit the melody

   v. what the lowest and highest notes of the piece are

b. Which of the indicators listed above is completely useless in determining key?

Exercise 2

The following are all beginnings of pieces. State the most likely key for each piece. Explain your choice of key.

(Don't forget that in most cases, the key is determined by the **harmony** associated with the given notes.)

a.

b.

c.

d.

e.

f.

g.

h.

i.

j.

B5 KEY AND TONALITY ANSWERS

Exercise 1

   a. iv

   b. i

Exercise 2

   a. D minor. The notes fit with the chords i, iv and V in D minor.

   b. F# minor. The notes fit with i and V(7) in F# minor.

   c. C# minor. The notes make a triad of C# minor.

   d. B minor. The notes fit with i and V in B minor.

   e. Db major. The notes fit I and IV in Db major.

   f. Eb major. The notes fit with V, I and IV in Eb major.

   g. F major. The B natural is a chromatic alteration (it doesn't affect the harmony) as it falls on a weak beat and is decorative. The notes fit I and IV/V7 in F major.

   h. The D# is a chromatic passing note. The notes fit I and V in G major.

   i. Eb minor. A nasty key signature, but the first bar makes the triad of Eb minor, and the second bar makes Ab minor, chord iv

   j. G minor. The notes fit i and V7 in G minor.

B6 MODULATION

What is Modulation?

"Modulation" is an important sounding word which just means "change of key". A modulation can happen with or without a change in **key signature**. In fact, most modulations don't require a change of key signature.

Generally the key signature is only changed when a significantly long portion of the piece is in a different key. Most often, the key changes only last for a certain number of bars, and then the melody returns to the tonic key (or modulates again).

You can sometimes tell that a piece has modulated when there are lots of accidentals on the page!

In the grade six music theory exam, modulation can happen in your composition in one of two ways:

- The melody will modulate towards the end and will **finish in the new key**. (In this case, your melody is in fact just a section of a larger, as yet unwritten, piece.)
- The modulation will happen at the end of the antecedent phrase, and will return to the original key by the end of the piece. (In this case, the piece itself is complete.)

In recent grade six music theory exam papers, there has been a choice of questions which is either to

- write a piece which **must** modulate and finish in the new key (i.e. is unfinished)
- write a piece which is **complete** (i.e. ends in the original key) with modulation optional.

The Mechanics of Modulation

Modulation is usually achieved through the combination of two techniques:

1. a pivot chord, followed by
2. a V-I progression in the new key

1. A pivot chord is one which exists in both the old and the new key. For example, the chord of C major exists in the key of C major as chord I, in G major as chord IV, in F major as chord V and in E minor as chord VI.

Let's say that our piece modulates from C major to G major (the dominant key).

The chords I, iii, V and vi in C major also exist in G major as IV, vi, I and ii.

	Chord: C major	**Chord: E minor**	**Chord: G major**	**Chord: A minor**
Key: C major	I	iii	V	vi
Key: G major	IV	vi	I	ii

You need to pick a pivot chord, then use it as a stepping stone to reach the new key.

2. The next step is to **confirm** the new key.

This is most effectively done by writing a V-I progression, with the leading note moving to the new tonic. For example, we write an F#-G in the melody. Remember we are now in G major, so the V-I progression is D major to G major. F# is outside of the C major scale, so using this note helps us to understand that we are in a new key.

It's always helpful to try to include any notes from the new key which **didn't exist** in the original one. If we modulate from C major to F major (to the sub-dominant), the leading note to tonic progression is not as striking as it was in the previous example, because the notes E-F exist in both C major and F major. However, we could include a Bb in our melody (for example, Bb-A-G-F as a falling scale), for a similar effect.

The dominant 7th chord is also very useful when you modulate, as often it contains a note which is alien to the old key. If you modulate from C major to F major, and you use V7-I, the V7 chord contains Bb, which could not occur in C major.

Choose your melody notes carefully - make sure there is no ambiguity of key by including notes which are **unique** to the new key and not present in the old one.

Where to Modulate to?

In the Grade Six music theory exam, the key you have to modulate to will be one of these four:

- to the dominant
- to the subdominant
- to the relative major
- to the relative minor

Of course, in real life it's possible to make your music modulate to any new key under the sun. You can make C major modulate to F# major, if you really want to! We will stick to these four for now though.

In all of these modulations, there will be **four** possible pivot chords, and only **one** note which needs to be chromatically altered in the new key (unless it's minor - see below!)

Here is a list of the pivot chords for each modulation:

Type of Modulation	Pivot Chords			
Tonic > Dominant (raise the 4th)	I > IV	iii > vi	V > I	vi > ii
Tonic > Subdominant (lower the 7th)	I > V	ii > vi	IV > I	vi > iii
Major > Minor (raise the 5th and maybe 4th)	ii > iv	IV > VI	vi > i	vii° > ii°
Minor > Major (lower the 7th)	iv > ii	VI > IV	i > vi	ii° > vii°

Examples:

- If you want to modulate from D major to the dominant key, A major, you could use chord V in D (A major) which would become chord I in A major. Include a raised 4th (=G#).

- If you want to modulate from C# minor to the relative major, E major, you could use chord iv in C# minor (F# minor) which would become chord ii in E major. Lower the 7th (=B natural from B#).

- If you modulate from C major to A minor, the relative minor, you could use chord vi in C major (A minor), which would become chord i in A minor. You should raise the 5th (G#), and might also have to raise the 4th (F#), if you're using an ascending melodic minor scale.

It's worth noting that some of these pivot chords are based on primary chords (I, IV or V). You will find them easier to use in most cases, because the primary chords are more effective at fixing the new key in our minds. (For the same reason that they are used at the beginning of a piece.)

You don't need to learn that table off by heart, by the way! The quick way to work out your pivot chords is to simply write out the letter names of the scale in the original key (e.g. A major):

A   B   C#   D   E   F#   G#

Then write the letter names of the new key directly underneath (we'll put the sub-dominant, D major):

Old key: A   B   C#   D   E   F#   G#

New key: A   B   C#   D   E   F#   G

Cross out the column which contains notes with a different accidental (G-G# here). The notes you have left can be used in triads in both keys.

There will be four triads – write them out so you don't forget them!

Examples

This is a complete piece – Gavotte from Suite No.6 by Richard Jones.

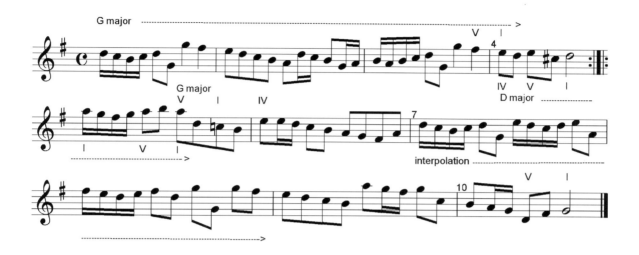

The key is G major.

- In bar 4, chord I of G major becomes the pivot chord IV of D major. (The E is an accented passing note).
- Chord V of D major is immediately introduced, consolidating the new key.
- The C#, which is not a note in G major, helps to fix the new key.
- The phrase ends with a perfect cadence in D major.
- The next section begins in D major, but the third beat of bar 5 is a pivot chord; I in D major or V in G major.
- The C natural helps to confirm that we are returning to the key of G major.
- It's also interesting to note the interpolation section in bars 7-8.
- The piece ends with a perfect cadence in G major.

Our second example is from the Haydn Andante we looked at earlier, when discussing cadences. We'll revisit it, to study how the modulations were achieved.

- The piece starts in Bb major, and the first phrase ends with an imperfect cadence in Bb major in bar 4.

- Bar 5 contains the pivot chord I in Bb major, which is IV in F major.

- Bar 6 is chord V in F major – the dominant key.

- The E naturals in bar 6 help to fix the key, and also create a V-I progression from bars 6-7.

- The section ends in the new key, with a perfect cadence. This is not the end of the piece. In the next section, the key will modulate back to Bb major.

B6 MODULATION EXERCISES

Exercise 1

a. What is a pivot chord?

b. fter choosing a pivot chord to *begin* a modulation, which chord progression should you use in order to *fix* the new key?

Exercise 2

For each of the following pairs of keys, name the **four** possible pivot chords by letter name, (e.g. "C major").

a. Bb major & F major:

b. Ab major and Db major:

c. Eb major and C minor:

d. C major and G major:

e. G# minor and B major:

f. E major and A major:

g. F# major and D# minor:

EXERCISE 3

Label the following simple melodies following the given example.

1. First, state the opening key, above the stave.
2. Above the stave, identify the notes which belong to the pivot chord and state the key the piece modulates to.
3. Below the stave on the marked lines, write the Roman numerals which correspond to the chords in those keys. The pivot chord should be labelled with the chord in both keys, using a slash (/).
4. State whether the modulation was to the dominant, subdominant, relative major or relative minor.

Example: modulates to the relative minor

B6 MODULATION ANSWERS

Exercise 1

a. A chord which exists in the original AND in the new key, and which is used to make a modulation to the new key.

b. V (or V7) – I (or i)

Exercise 2

a. Bb major, D minor, F major, G minor

b. Ab major, Bb minor, Db major, F minor

c. F minor, Ab major, C minor, D diminished

d. C major, E minor, G major, A minor

e. G# minor, A# diminished, C# minor, E major

f. E major, F# minor, A major, C# minor

g. G# minor, B major, D# minor, E# diminished

Exercise 3

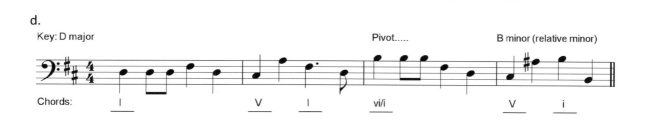

B7 HOW TO COMPOSE

Lessons B1-B6 have covered the basics of how compositions are made. The next step is to combine all these elements together and begin to craft your own compositions.

At this point we need to stress that you are composing **as part of a music theory exam** – not for a composition exam! In order to get a high score, you need to demonstrate that you know how a composition is structured by putting theory into practice. You don't get high marks for showing a lot of imagination or by breaking away from the established rules. As in most areas of art, you need to learn the rules before you break them.

So the best way to begin your composition is by **reviewing the given opening**, and then **making a plan**. After that you can do the **composing**, then finish off by **polishing**.

Reviewing the given opening

- Check the key and time signature of the opening.
- Look at the rhythms, motifs and sequences and decide which elements are **characteristic** of the piece.
- Check the length. It will usually be two full bars, but not always.

Making a Plan

- Decide on the overall length of your composition.
- Decide on the length of the antecedent and consequent phrases. Decide whether you will include an interpolation section.
- Plan your modulations (if any).
- Plan your cadences.

You're now ready to compose!

Composing

- Make minor modifications to the given material to complete the antecedent phrase. Think about sequencing and reusing motifs. Try to use 2-bar sections.
- Make sure your melody fits a suitable cadence (and possible modulation) at the end of the antecedent phrase.
- Make minor modifications to the antecedent phrase to make the consequent phrase.
- Don't forget to include an interpolation if you want to.
- Make sure the consequent phrase ends on a perfect cadence in the right key.

Polishing

- Double check that the instrument which you've written for can actually play the notes you've written. This shouldn't be a problem unless you've written very low or very high notes. Don't forget that the flute cannot play lower than middle C, and the oboe's lowest note is Bb below middle C.

- Add in performance instructions. You should indicate the dynamics, phrasing and articulation and maybe also expression. Articulation is especially important for all wind instruments – the players need to know whether each note should be attacked with the tongue or not. Use phrase marks to show which notes should be played in one breath or sweep of the bow. Make sure your wind player has somewhere to breathe! You can add bowing marks to string music if they add something to the piece musically - don't just add them for the sake of it though.

- Double check that you have not made any silly mistakes like writing the wrong number of beats in a bar. In particular, if the piece started on an up-beat, make sure the last bar contains the right number of beats.

- Sing your melody through in your head, quite slowly. Make any adjustments or improvements which seem necessary.

EXAMPLE ANSWERS WITH COMMENTARY

"Continue this opening to form a complete melody for unaccompanied flute. It should end with a modulation to the relative minor and should be between eight and ten bars long. Add performance directions as appropriate."

1. Review the Opening.

- It's in A major. (The question tells us to modulate to the relative minor, so we know it must be major!)

- It's in 4/4 time.

- The first bar is basically a falling tonic triad with an added B as an auxiliary note. There is a leap of an octave. The second bar moves by step for the first two beats with F# as another auxiliary note, then there is a falling perfect 4th.

- The section is 2 bars long. The next section will start on the last beat of the second bar. The final bar will have three beats in it.

2. Make a plan

- I will decide to write a 10-bar composition. The antecedent phrase will be 4 bars long, and the consequent will be 6 bars and contain an interpolation section.

- The music has to modulate to F# minor by the end.

- The given opening appears to end on a V chord, so the antecedent should probably end on I, in order to prevent repetition.

- I will make the music modulate in bar 9. D major is a pivot chord, because it is IV in A major, and VI in F# minor. The end of the piece will be a perfect cadence, C# major to F# minor.

- I can write out my plan like this:

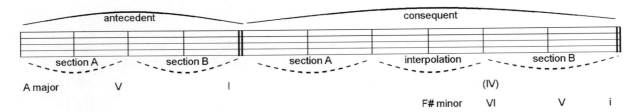

- Notice how the piece is now **completely structured**, with ordered phrase and section lengths, sensible cadences and a suitable modulation.

  When you are awarded points in the grade six music theory exam, this is what the examiner will be looking for. Having a pretty tune is an advantage of course, but the foundation of your composition is very important.

3. Composing

First I need to complete the antecedent phrase. Because the first bar would be harmonised with chord I, and the phrase will end on chord V, I'll use notes which are part of the chord IV to add some variety. I'll adapt the quaver (8th note) rhythm from bar 2, using the notes of the D major chord moving in small steps, and then using the notes of the A major chord moving through the triad.

I'll then add a big leap of a 10th up to high C#, in an echo of the octave leap in bar 1. This is a piece for flute, which is quite at home playing in that register.

I'll start the section after a quaver (8th) rest, which will give the flautist a chance to catch his/her breath.

Next I'll take the motif starting from the first beat of bar 1 and write a sequence which starts one step lower down the scale.

This means my section ends on G#, which also fits chord V, making an imperfect cadence at the end of the phrase.

The next section is the start of the consequent phrase. I need to develop the material from section A first.

Again I give the flute player a quaver (8th) rest. I'll start the next section on G#, because the previous section started on a repeated note after the rest (E).

I use the same rhythm from bar 1, and use the notes from the same chord (I).

However, in bar 1 the figure starts on C#, so I'll start on A for variety. Instead of leaping up an octave, I'll go up a 4th to A, and move smoothly by step to make bar 6 a sequence of bar 2, starting a 3rd higher.

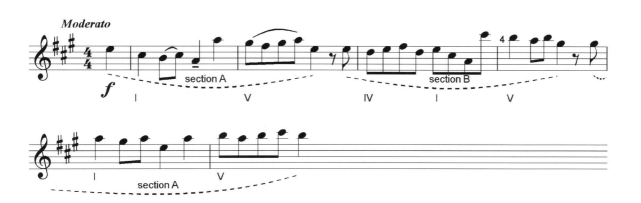

Next comes the interpolation. There should be in increase in drama, so I'll make the melody continue to rise. I can do this by putting the opening up one octave starting on the E.

Again, instead of the octave leap, I'll put a leap of a 4th, which is similar to the end of bar 5. This is also helpful, because it suggests the chord of D major at the end of bar 8, which is the pivot chord we need in order to modulate to F# minor.

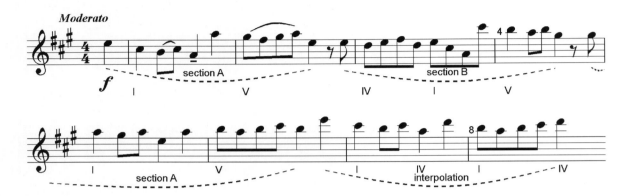

Finally we need to write the last section based on section B.

We assume that chord IV in A major is now VI in F# minor. We need the notes in the next bar to fit chord V (C# minor), so that we can incorporate a perfect cadence and also to include the E# which will help to fix the new key, because it's a note which doesn't exist in the old key.

I'll base the melody on bar 3, but invert the first half of the bar, for a little variety.

The second half of the bar is similar in that it's a falling triad. At this point I add the octave leap (up to C#).

The final bar is a sequence of bar 4.

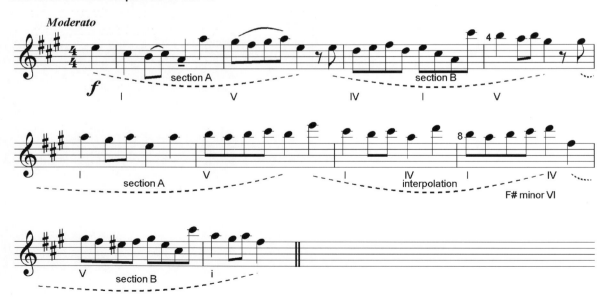

4. Polishing

All the notes would be easy to play on a flute.

However, I need to look carefully at the end of each section. In some places there is a quaver (8th) rest, in others there is not. We need to be consistent, while bearing in mind that the player needs to breathe.

Since the first note of the piece is a crotchet (quarter note), I think it will be better to start both phrases with a crotchet (quarter note). However, I can begin the two section Bs with a quaver (8th).

I need to change bars 4 and 8 accordingly.

I need to add some phrasing, articulation, dynamics and breathing marks.

I will try to keep the phrasing and articulation of similar patterns consistent throughout. The piece will start loud, become softer, then crescendo during the interpolation, finishing again quite loud.

I use commas to show suggested breathing places.

B7 COMPOSING EXERCISES

On the following two pages you will find a selection of openings to make into finished compositions.

Read the instructions for each question carefully, and complete the "preparation task" before you begin each time.

Preparation Task:
- What key is it in?
- What is the time signature?
- What instrument are you writing for?
- Exactly how many bars are you going to write? Is there an upbeat to take into account? (Will you include an interpolation section?)
- Will you include a modulation, if so to what key? What key will you end in? What are the pivot chords in those two keys?
- Which parts of the opening are interesting enough to be used as motifs throughout the piece?
- Is the given opening exactly two bars long? (If not, what do you need to consider?)
- What cadences are you going to imply and what bar/beat will they fall on?

1. Continue this opening for unaccompanied clarinet to make a complete piece of not less than eight bars in length. You may make any modulation or modulations that you wish, or none if you prefer.

Add performance directions as appropriate.

2. Continue this opening for unaccompanied cello to make a complete piece of not less than eight bars in length. You may make any modulation or modulations that you wish, or none if you prefer.

Add performance directions as appropriate.

3. Continue this opening for unaccompanied flute to make a complete melody of not less than eight bars in length. Include a modulation to the relative minor and end in the new key.

Add performance directions as appropriate.

4. Continue this opening for unaccompanied bassoon to make a complete melody of not less than eight bars in length. Include a modulation to the dominant and end in the new key.

Add performance directions as appropriate.

B7 COMPOSING ANSWERS

The following are example answers – many answers are possible.

1. (F minor)

Make sure you have re-used the semiquaver (16th note) figure from bar 1, with the lower auxiliary note. The last bar should contain 5 quavers' (8th notes') worth of notes.

2. (A major)

Make sure you have used 3/2 rhythms throughout, and have not slipped into 6/4 (i.e. you need three clear beats per bar). Re-use the dotted rhythm, and try to use some more large leaps similar to the leap of a 7th in bar 1.

3. (F major modulating to D minor)

Modulate to D minor using a pivot chord, followed by V then i. In this model answer, the pivot chord is IV/VI (Bb major) at the end of bar 6, which is followed by A and C# (V), then i (D). Don't forget that the lowest note on the flute is middle C.

4. (G major modulating to D major)

Here the modulation takes place in bar 6 with the pivot I/V (D major) followed by A major (V), then D major (chord I) in bar 7. Make sure that the melody includes C#, as the only note which exists in D major but not in G major. Re-use the rhythm with the rest, and the syncopated element from bar 2 (the crotchet (quarter note) G falls on a weak beat).

C1A READING AN ORCHESTRAL SCORE

The grade six music theory exam paper normally contains two separate, full-page musical scores. The questions you are asked are very varied, and this part of the grade six course will help you to answer any question which might come up.

The first step in answering any of these questions though, is being able to read the score itself!

You can expect to find a score for any **combination** and any **number** of instruments. Usually, one of the scores will be for a full orchestra, and the other will be for a smaller group of players, for example a piano, cello and voice, or a string quartet.

You will have to bear in mind that some of the musical parts are for transposing instruments, and they will not be written at concert pitch. You'll have to be able to read the viola's alto clef, and the tenor clef is likely to crop up too.

This means that if you are, for example, asked to describe a chord played by the full orchestra, you will need to simultaneously transpose some notes and read some awkward clefs. With practice though, it's not as hard as it sounds!

Let's get started by dissecting an orchestral score.

ORCHESTRAL MUSIC

Symphonies and concertos are examples of **orchestral music**. A full symphony orchestra can have up to 90 or more musicians. The majority of them are string players, with a much smaller number of woodwind, brass and percussion players.

A symphony is a piece written for the whole orchestra with no particular soloist. A concerto is a piece written for one (or sometimes more) solo instrument, and the orchestra provides an accompaniment.

Here is the first page of the full orchestral score of Beethoven's 5th Symphony. These are the first 11 eleven bars.

Notice how the score is laid out:

- Each stave is labelled on the left with the name of the instrument which plays it.

- Woodwind and brass instruments are **preceded** by a number (e.g. 2 Fagotti) – this is the **number of players** who should read and play from one stave. Often there are two flutes, two oboes, two clarinets and two bassoons, for example. But there will only be one flute stave, one oboe stave, one clarinet stave and one bassoon stave. Both players' parts are written on the **same stave**. (This saves space!)

- Instruments are sometimes **followed** by a number, I, II etc. (e.g. Violino I). This is not the number of actual players, but shows that there is a **second (or more) stave assigned** to that instrument. In the Beethoven score above, there is a part for Violin I and Violin II. In fact, around 12 violinists will play stave I, and another 10 or so violinists will play stave II.

- When there is one solo instrument plus orchestra, it is often marked as "principale".

- Expect to find the instrument names in Italian, German or French, depending on the nationality of the composer.

- The instruments are always written in the same order from top to bottom.

- The woodwind instruments are at the top, followed by the brass, followed by the percussion, followed by the strings.

- Each **family** of instruments is grouped together with a **square bracket** on the left – notice how the first square bracket connects the flute, oboe, clarinet and bassoon parts.

- When two or more staves belong to the same kind of instrument, they are connected with a **brace** (e.g. the Violino I and II parts above).

- Bar lines are usually drawn through all the wind and percussion parts, and then through the string parts. You might see variations on this, however.

- Staves are connected together like this to create a "**system**". This system contains 12 separate staves.

- This is the first page of the score, so all the instruments are included even if they have nothing but rests. In subsequent systems, the names of the instruments may be left off or abbreviated, and staves which contain nothing but rests are not included. This saves paper when a symphony is printed!

- The name of any transposing instruments usually (but not always) includes the note which sounds at concert pitch when the player reads the note C. (E.g. "Clarinetti in B" here is Italian for "clarinets in B flat". This means that a written C sounds at concert pitch Bb. For more about why B=Bb, see Lesson C2b Musical Instruments.)

- Brass parts are sometimes written without a key signature, as here. Accidentals are written instead.

The next page of the Beethoven score looks like this:

The instrument names are sometimes abbreviated, or omitted completely, as here. Use the brackets to help work out which stave belongs to which instrument.

Where instruments share a stave, there are three possible scenarios:

1. There are **two different parts on one stave**. In the flute part in bar 18, the first flute will play the higher notes, and the second player takes the lower notes. This is sometimes marked in the score as "div." or "divisi", meaning "divided". Sometimes when parts overlap, one note is written with two stems, one pointing up and the other pointing down. In the flute part bar 20, both players should play the C.

2. There is **one part on one stave** for all/both players. In the horn part in bar 18, it is marked "zu 2", which means "both players". In Italian this is written as "a 2". In French it is "a deux". A string part may be marked as "unis." which stands for "unison", meaning all the string players should play that single part.

3. Only **one** player should play the part. In this case, you will see the word "solo".

Following an Orchestral Score

It's easy to feel a bit overwhelmed when you look at orchestral scores for the first time. But don't panic – here are some tips to help you get more familiar with them:

Remember that many instruments are likely to be playing more or less the same notes. In bar 22 of the Beethoven, the orchestra is playing **in unison**, which means everybody is playing the same notes (although in different octaves!)

Often, the fast moving notes will be the melody, whereas the harmony will be written with slower note values (this is a generalisation though).

You can browse through many orchestral scores for free. Visit http://imslp.org/wiki/Main_Page and search for symphonies or concertos. This is a legal database of out-of-copyright musical scores in pdf format. Use Youtube.com to find recordings of any scores you find, and try to follow them as the music is playing. Try to follow the stave for one particular instrument. Start with something easy (a slow movement, an instrument you are familiar with) and as you get more confident, try faster pieces or staves with tricky clefs or for transposing instruments.

Saving Space

Some short-cuts are used in scores to save on space and printing costs. In a score, any parts in a system which consist entirely of rests will not be printed. If an instrument seems to have disappeared from your score, it will be taking a rest!

When parts contain several repeated fast notes, these are often written as **measured quavers (eighth notes)** or **measured semiquavers (16th notes)** etc. An appropriate number of slashes is drawn through the tail of a longer note, like this:

The two slashes on each note mean that the value of note to play is a semiquaver (16th note), so this bar actually contains sixteen Gs. Don't confuse this with a **tremolo** – it's not the same. A tremolo may be indicated with this symbol, but will also use the word "tremolo" or "trem." Notes in a tremolo are **unmeasured** rhythmically.

C1A READING AN ORCHESTRAL SCORE EXERCISES

Look at the extract from Mozart's Symphony no. 25 in G minor on the next page, and answer the questions below.

1. How many types of woodwind instrument are playing in this extract?

2. How many oboe players are there?

3. What is the concert pitch of the notes played by the horn in G in bar 5?

4. Which two different instruments share a stave? (Give their English names.)

5. True or False: The first and second violins play in unison throughout this extract?

6. Which orchestral section (family) does not feature in this movement?

7. How many systems are there on this page?

8. In this extract, the violas are playing: "a deux", "divisi" or "unis."?

9. Why does the notated G in bar 9 of the "Corni in G" part have two stems?

10. What is "Corni in B" in English?

C1A READING AN ORCHESTRAL SCORE ANSWERS

1. One (the oboe).

2. Two (notice the "2" written above the stave).

3. G (if an instrument is in G, then a written C will sound as a G).

4. Cello and double bass.

5. True.

6. Percussion.

7. Two (a system is a complete, joined up unit of staves. Individual systems are separated by two short diagonal lines).

8. Unis. ("Unis"="in unison", or all together. "a2" is used when only two players share a part, and "divisi" is used when one stave is split into two parts.)

9. Because it's played by two horns at the same time.

10. French horns in Bb. (B in German is Bb in English. Mozart used this because he spoke German. You can also work this out from the key signature – compare with the staves for an instrument which doesn't transpose.)

C1B READING A CHAMBER MUSIC SCORE

"Chamber music" is any music written for a small number of players – it can be performed in your living room, if you can find the necessary musicians! Common chamber music formats include the sonata, string quartet and lied (pronounced "leed"), but in fact any combination of instruments and singers is possible.

A **sonata** is a piece for a solo instrument with a piano accompaniment. A **string quartet** is written for two violins, a viola and a cello. A **lied** is a piece for voice and piano. Lieder (the plural of "lied" is "lieder") were made popular by Schubert in the 19th century.

Chamber music scores follow the same principal as orchestral scores. Instruments are written in the same order as they would appear in an orchestral score. When there is an instrumental or voice part plus piano, the piano part is written underneath.

Look at the score on the following page, which is the first page of a Quintet for piano, oboe, clarinet, horn and bassoon by Mozart (KV 452). It contains two systems.

Notice the following points:

- The clarinet part is written for a Bb clarinet, transposed (Clarinetto in B).
- The horn part is written for horn in Eb (Corno in Es).
- Fagotto is Italian for bassoon.
- A piano part is always written on a double stave, joined with a curved bracket on the left.
- Unless otherwise marked, the pianist plays the top stave with his right hand, and the lower stave with his left. Occasionally, the player is instructed to "cross hands", i.e. the left hand crosses over the right hand to play high notes, or the right hand crosses the left to play lower notes. This is written in the score as r.h. (right hand) or l.h. (left hand) in English. In Italian, you will see m.s. (mano sinistra) for left hand, or m.d. (mano destra) for right hand.
- In a piano part, the upper stave is usually in treble clef, and the lower stave is bass clef. However, if particularly high or low notes are needed, the clefs can be changed. In the Mozart score, the left hand starts in the bass clef. In the same bar, a treble clef is then written so that the next three quavers can be written neatly (without lots of ledger lines). The clef changes to bass clef again – the new clef is written before the bar line when the clef change applies to the next bar. Look closely at the score and see how many clef changes you can spot in the left hand piano part.

142

Voice parts are easy to spot – they have words written underneath! Sometimes the voice is labelled as "tenor" or "soprano" etc., sometimes a name is given e.g. "Esmeralda", sometimes it is simply labelled "voice".

Here is the beginning of a song called "Abendlied der Furstin" ("Evening Song of the Princess") by Schubert:

- The voice part is labelled "Singstimme", which means "singing voice". Notice how the piano right-hand part starts in the bass clef, although a treble clef is placed at the beginning of the line. Always be on the lookout for changes of clef!

C1B READING A CHAMBER MUSIC SCORE EXERCISES

1. Which of the following types of composition normally fall into the category "chamber music" (choose all that apply)?

    1. Sonata
    2. Symphony
    3. Quintet
    4. Concerto
    5. Lied

2. Answer "True" or "False" for these statements about the **piano:**

    a. The upper stave is *usually* played by the right hand.
    b. The lower stave *always* uses the bass clef.
    c. The letters m.s. indicate that the player should use his/her *left hand*.
    d. It is possible to have the same clef on both staves.
    e. *Occasionally* the alto clef is used for the right hand.
    f. *Occasionally* piano music is written on three, rather than two, staves.
    g. The clef of a stave can only change at the beginning of a line of music.

3. Look at the extract on the next page, which is the beginning of Schubert's Quintet in A Major, Op.114 ("The Trout Quintet") and answer the questions.

    a. What is the lowest note played by the viola in this extract?
    b. Bar 1 of the cello/double bass part contains a crotchet (quarter note) and a semibreve (whole note) - explain which instrument should play which note and why.
    c. Explain "8va............" in bars 15-17 of the piano part.
    d. What is the letter name of the last note in this extract played in the left hand piano part?
    e. How many violins play in the first bar of the piece?
    f. True or False: in bar 7, the violin and cello play in unison.

C1B READING A CHAMBER MUSIC SCORE ANSWERS

1. Sonata, Quintet and Lied

2.

- a. True (usually, but not always)
- b. False (it can use either the bass or treble clef)
- c. True (m.s. stands for "mano sinistra" which is "left hand" in Italian)
- d. True (this is very common)
- e. False (the C clefs are never used on in piano music)
- f. True (music which spans a large range of the keyboard is sometimes written like this)
- g. False (the clef can change at any point)

3.

- a. A below middle C
- b. The cello plays the crotchet (quarter note) A, while the double bass plays the semibreve (whole note) A. The stem is pointing upward on the crotchet (quarter note), which means it is the upper part = cello part.
- c. The notes marked "8va............" should be played an octave higher.
- d. G natural. (Did you spot the treble clef?!)
- e. One. (Chords can be played on a violin.)
- f. False. They have different melodies.

C2A INSTRUMENTS, FAMILIES AND NAMES

For the grade six music theory exam you need to know several facts about musical instruments. You will need to know:

- which are the standard instruments in each family, and which other instruments are commonly used in a symphony orchestra
- the names of the instruments in Italian, German and French, including the plural forms and abbreviations (you only need to be able to recognise the names, not give them)
- what key(s) transposing instruments are in, and how these keys are written in other languages
- which instruments use a single or double reed to produce sound
- what note each string is tuned to, for string instruments

We'll look at each of these points in turn.

a. **Orchestral Families.** The orchestra is divided into four families, the woodwind, brass, percussion and strings. The standard instruments and additional optional orchestral instruments in each family are:

- **Woodwind** – flute, oboe, clarinet and bassoon; *plus* piccolo, cor Anglais, bass clarinet, Eb clarinet and contrabassoon.
- **Brass** – trumpet, French horn, trombone and tuba; *plus* bass trombone
- **Percussion** – timpani, snare drum, bass drum, cymbals, triangle; *plus* tambourine, glockenspiel, xylophone and gong
- **Strings** – violin, viola, cello and double bass; *plus* harp

b. **Instrument Names.** Many instrument names in Italian, German and French are quite similar to the English – or close enough for you to be able to work out.

Some of them are, on the other hand, completely different. These are the ones you need to memorise!

Here are two tables of vocabulary – table 1 is "Easy" and table 2 is "Learn Me!"

Table 1 – Easy

English	Italian	German	French
Flute	Flauto	Flöte	Flûte
Piccolo	Flauto piccolo	Kleine flöte	Petite flûte
Oboe	Oboe	Hoboe	Hautbois*
English horn	Corno inglese	Englischhorn	Cor anglais
Clarinet	Clarinetto	Klarinette	Clarinette
Bass clarinet	Clarinetto basso	Bassklarinette	Clarinette basse
Horn	Corno	Horn	Cor
Tuba	Tuba	Tuba	Tuba
Triangle	Triangolo	Triangel	Triangle
Tambourine	Tamburello	Tamburin	Tambour de Basque
Xylophone	Xilofono	Xylophon	Xylophone
Gong	Gong	Gong	Gong
Violin	Violino	Violine	Violon
Cello	Violoncello	Violoncello	Violoncello
Double bass	Contrabasso or basso	Kontrabass	Contrebass

*the "h" and the "t" are silent, so in fact this is pronounced "obwa".

Table 2 – Learn Me!

The words in **bold** are the ones which are likely to cause confusion!

English	Italian	German	French
Bassoon	**Fagotto**	**Fagott**	Basson
Double bassoon or contrabassoon	**Contrafagotto**	**Kontrafagott**	Contrebasson
Trumpet	**Tromba****	Trompete	Trompette
Trombone	Trombone	**Posaune**	Trombone
Kettle drums	Timpani	**Pauken**	**Timbales**
Side drum or snare drum	**Tamburo piccolo**	**Kleine Trommel**	**Caisse claire**
Bass drum	**Cassa** or **gran cassa**	**Grosse Trommel**	**Grosse caisse**
Cymbals	**Piatti** or **cinelli**	**Becken**	Cymbales
Glockenspiel	**Campanelli**	Glockenspiel	**Jeu de timbres**
Viola	Viola	**Bratsche**	**Alto**

** Do not confuse Tromba with Trombone!

C2A INSTRUMENTS, FAMILIES AND NAMES EXERCISES

Test 1

1. Which instrument is missing from this list of the standard four orchestral string instruments: violin, cello, double bass?

2. Which orchestral families do each of these instruments belong to?

    a. Cor Anglais
    b. Double bass
    c. Timpani
    d. Tambourine
    e. Piccolo
    f. Contrabassoon
    g. Viola

3. Give the English name for each of these instruments:

    a. Fagotto
    b. Kontrabass
    c. Posaune
    d. Caisse claire
    e. Tamburin
    f. Grosse Trommel
    g. Piatti
    h. Jeu de timbres
    i. Hoboe
    j. Violon
    k. Alto
    l. Trompete

TEST 2

1. Which instrument is missing from this list of the standard four orchestral brass instruments: trumpet, trombone, tuba?

2. Which instrument is missing from this list of the standard four orchestral woodwind instruments: flute, clarinet, bassoon?

3. Which orchestral families do each of these instruments belong to?

    a. Harp

    b. Kettle drums

    c. French horn

    d. Gong

    e. Trombone

4. Give the English name for each of these instruments:

    a. Contrebasson

    b. Xilifono

    c. Tambourino

    d. Grosse caisse

    e. Pauken

    f. Tamburo piccolo

    g. Campanelli

    h. Tromba

    i. Clarinetto basso

    j. Hautbois

    k. Bratsche

    l. Basson

    m. Becken

C2A INSTRUMENTS, FAMILIES AND NAMES ANSWERS

Test 1

1. Viola

2.
   a. Woodwind
   b. Strings
   c. Percussion
   d. Percussion
   e. Woodwind
   f. Woodwind
   g. Strings

3.
   a. Bassoon
   b. Double bass
   c. Trombone
   d. Snare drum (or side drum)
   e. Tambourine
   f. Bass drum
   g. Cymbals
   h. Glockenspiel
   i. Oboe
   j. Violin
   k. Viola
   l. Trumpet

Test 2

1. French horn

2. Oboe

3.
   a. Strings
   b. Percussion
   c. Brass
   d. Percussion
   e. Brass

4.
   a. Double bassoon (or contrabassoon)
   b. Xylophone
   c. Tambourine
   d. Bass drum
   e. Kettle drums (or timpani)
   f. Snare drum (or side drum)
   g. Glockenspiel
   h. Trumpet
   i. Bass clarinet
   j. Oboe
   k. Viola
   l. Bassoon
   m. Cymbals

C2B TRANSPOSING, STRING AND REED INSTRUMENTS

c. **Transposing Instruments.** The clarinet, cor Anglais, trumpet and French horn are transposing instruments. The note which actually sounds at concert pitch when the player reads/plays the note C determines what pitch the instrument is "in". For each of these instruments, the concert pitch note is **lower** than the written note.

- Clarinets are usually in Bb or A.
- The cor Anglais is in F.
- The trumpet is usually in Bb.
- The French horn is usually in F.

In addition, you should note the following:

- The bass clarinet is in Bb and sounds a major 9th lower than written (one octave lower than the Bb clarinet).

- There is a smaller version of the clarinet in Eb, which sounds a minor 3rd **higher** than written. The French horn is also sometimes found in Eb, sounding a minor 3rd higher than written.

- Trumpets can be found in other keys, such as C (non-transposing), or D (sounding a major second higher than written).

- The piccolo sounds one octave **higher** than written.

- The double bassoon sounds one octave **lower** than written.

- The most commonly used size of trombone is the "tenor trombone", which is sometimes called the Bb trombone. However, it is not treated as a transposing instrument in orchestral scores, and its notes sound as written.

- The double bass sounds one octave **lower** than written.

You also need to know that the letter names we use for the notes (A-G), and the names "sharp" and "flat", are translated in different ways.

English	A	Bb	F	Eb	D
Italian/French	La	Si bemolle/bémol	Fa	Mi bemolle/bémol	Re
German	A	B	F	Es	D

- The English note B is called H in German. (J. S. Bach used to "sign" his manuscripts with the notes B-A-C-H, which would be Bb-A-C-B in English!)

- You may see "Klarinette in B" on a score – don't forget that it means "clarinet in Bb"!

- You may find it useful to learn the sol-fa names for the notes C-B: Do, re, mi, fa, so(l) la, ti (or si). Learn the Do-Re-Mi song!

d. **Reeds.** The oboe, cor Anglais, clarinet and bassoon are reed instruments (as are the larger/smaller versions of these instruments). The clarinet uses a single reed, but the others all use a double reed.

e. **Open Strings.** When a string player plays a note without pressing a finger down anywhere on the string, this is called an "open note". If the player touches the string, the vibrating length of the string is shortened and the note produced is higher.

The note produced by the open string is the lowest note possible on that string, and it is the note which the string is tuned to.

You need to know what notes are produced on the open strings for each of the four string instruments. You might be asked, for example, to circle in a score a note which could be played on an open string. So, you need to know not only the letter **name**, but also which **octave** the note is in.

Here are the notes which the string instrument strings are tuned to:

- Notice that the viola and cello are tuned to the same notes, except the cello is an octave lower.

- Notice that the violin, viola and cello are tuned in 5ths, but the double bass is tuned in 4ths.

- Don't forget that the double bass sounds an octave lower than written.

- It might help you to remember these tunings if you notice that the double bass strings are the same as the violin's in **reverse order**!

f. **Bowing Indications.** String instruments can produce many types of sound, depending on the exact method of making the strings vibrate. You need to learn some of the more common bowing directions.

- **Arco** is the normal bowing method. This word is only used after a different method has been indicated beforehand, and is the "default" method.

- **Pizzicato** means "plucked". The player plucks the string with his/her finger. Usually this is abbreviated to "pizz." The effect is short, pingy notes.

- **Sul ponticello** means "on the bridge". The player bows the part of the string on the other side of the instrument's bridge. The effect is a shimmery sound. Sometimes this is abbreviated to "sul pont."

- **Spiccato** means "bouncing". The bow is bounced off the strings.

- **Tremolo** is a rapid up and down movement of the bow, to create a mysterious or eerie effect. The notes are unmeasured, not played rhythmically. This is often abbreviated to "trem."

- **Col legno** means "with the wood" and is an instruction for the player to turn the bow upside down and play with the wooden side instead of the hair side.

- **Double corde** means "two strings" and is a direction to use "**double stopping**". This means the player has to use two strings at the same time. Triple stopping is also possible.

C2B TRANSPOSING, STRING AND REED EXERCISES

Exercise A

Answer the following questions:

a. In which two keys are standard clarinets normally found?

b. In which key do we normally find a small-sized clarinet?

c. Does the bass clarinet normally use the treble clef or the bass clef?

d. In what key is the cor Anglais?

e. Which two brass instruments are normally transposing?

f. At what pitch does a piccolo **sound**, compared to how it is written?

g. And the double bass?

h. Is the viola a transposing instrument?

i. What is "Tromba in B" in English?

j. What is "Klarinette in Mi Bemolle" in English?

k. What is "Corno in Re" in English?

Exercise B

Look at the extract on the next page, which is the first page of Beethoven's Symphony no.2, Op.36, and answer the questions which follow.

1. Which instruments in this piece are NOT transposing instruments?

2. Write out the bar 1 of the trumpet part, as it would sound at concert pitch. Include the new key signature. Use the treble clef.

3. For each of the string instruments, say whether the notes played in bar 1 can be played on an open string or not.

   a. Violin

   b. Viola

   c. Cello

4. Which instruments playing in this extract are **double** reed instruments?

5. True or false: The viola and horns are playing in unison in bar 1.

6. Which two standard orchestral brass instruments do not feature in this extract?

C. For each of the four standard orchestral string instruments, write out their four **open strings**.

C2B TRANSPOSING, STRING AND REEDS ANSWERS

Exercise A

a. Bb and A

b. Eb

c. Treble clef

d. F

e. Trumpet and French horn.

f. One octave higher.

g. One octave lower.

h. No.

i. Trumpet in Bb.

j. Clarinet in Eb.

k. Horn in D.

Exercise B

1. The flutes, oboes, bassoons, timpani, violins, violas and cellos.

2.

3.
   a. Yes
   b. Yes
   c. Yes

4. The oboes and bassoons.

5. True.

6. Trombone and tuba.

C.

C3 MUSICAL TERMS AND SIGNS

You can expect just about any musical term or symbol to crop up in a grade six music theory exam! Here is a list of terms, organised into groups. However, it's almost impossible to make a "complete" list of terms for this level.

Always check the meaning of any new term you come across when you are playing music.

1. Tempo — from very slow to very fast

Italian			
Larghissimo	Very, very slow	*Andantino*	At a moderate walking pace
Grave	Slow and solemn	*Moderato*	Moderately
Lento	Slowly	*Allegretto*	Moderately fast
Largo	Broadly	*Allegro*	Fast and bright
Larghetto	Rather broadly	*Vivace*	Fast and lively
Adagio	Slow and stately	*Vivacissimo*	Very fast and lively
Adagietto	Rather slow	*Presto*	Very fast
Andante	At a walking pace	*Prestissimo*	Extremely fast

French			
Grave	Slowly and solemnly	Rapide	Fast
Lent	Slowly	Vif	Lively
Modéré	Moderately	Vite	Fast

German			
Langsam	Slowly	*Lebhaft*	Lively
Mässig	Moderately	*Rasch*	Quickly
Bewegt	Animated	*Schnell*	Fast

2. Changes in tempo

Italian			
Accelerando	Speeding up	*Allargando*	Growing broader
Doppio movimento	Twice as fast	*Calando*	Going slower
Più mosso	More movement	*Meno mosso*	Less movement
Precipitando	Hurrying	*Rallentando*	Gradually slowing
Stretto	In a faster tempo	*Ritardando*	Slowing
Stringendo	Pressing on faster	*Ritenuto*	Slightly slower

French			
Plus vite	Faster	*Moins vite*	Less fast

3. Bowing Directions

There are a lot of different ways a string player can use a bow.
The more common bowing instructions should be learnt for grade six music theory:

Bowing Directions	
Arco	With the bow
Spiccato	Bounce the bow
Sul ponticello	Play near the bridge
Con sordino	With the mute
(notation: V symbol above note)	Up bow
Col legno	With the wood of the bow
Tremolo	Move the bow up and down extremely fast
Pizzicato	Pluck the strings
Senza sordino	Without the mute
(notation: ⊓ symbol above note)	Down bow

4. Mood

Italian			
Affettuoso	With feeling	*Lamentoso*	Mournfully
Agitato	Agitated	*Leggero*	Lightly
Appassionato	Passionately	*Maestoso*	Majestically
Animato	Animated	*Malinconico*	Melancholically
Brillante	Sparkling	*Marcato*	Marked
Bravura	Boldly	*Marziale*	In a military style
Cantabile	In a singing style	*Mesto*	Sadly
Dolce	Sweetly	*Morendo*	Dying
Energico	Energetically	*Nobilmente*	Nobly
Eroico	Heroically	*Patetico*	With emotion
Espressivo	Expressively	*Pesante*	Heavily
Furioso	Angrily	*Saltando*	Jumping
Giocoso	Merrily	*Scherzando*	Playfully
Gioioso	Joyfully	*Sostenuto*	Sustained
Grandioso	Grandly	*Tenerezza*	Tenderness
Grazioso	Gracefully	*Tranquillamente*	Calmly
Lacrimoso	Sadly	*Trionfante*	Triumphantly

5. Other Symbols

The following symbols also need to be learnt:

Other Symbols	
	Arpeggio (broken chord). The lowest note is played first, followed by the second, third etc., in quick succession.
	Tremolo (rapidly repeated note). Short diagonal lines across the stem of a note (or notes) show that it should be rapidly repeated. Often you will see "trem." written above the note as well. A tremolo is a kind of special effect.
	Measured semiquavers. This is a shorthand way of writing out semiquavers or other fast notes. The beams show you which note value is intended. Although it looks similar to a tremolo, it doesn't sound like one and there is no "trem."
	Glissando or **portamento** (rapidly play the notes between the two notated). This is sometimes seen in piano or trombone music. The musician plays all the notes in between the two notated notes as fast as possible.
	Stopped note. Used for the French horn, this cross instructs the player to move his/her hand further into the instrument's bell to create a muffled sound.

C3 MUSICAL TERMS AND SIGNS EXERCISES

Test 1

Give the English meaning of these terms and signs.

1. Allargando
2. Andantino
3. Arco
4. Bewegt
5. Brillante
6. Calando
7. Col legno
8. Con sordino
9. Dolce
10. Doppio movimento
11. Eroico
12. Gioioso
13. Lamentoso
14. Larghissimo
15. Mässig
16. Meno mosso
17. Moins vite
18. Morendo
19. Pesante
20. Precipitando
21. Schnell
22. Sostenuto
23. Spiccato
24. Vif
25.

Test 2

Give the English meaning of these terms and signs.

1. Agitato
2. Bravura
3. Cantabile
4. Giocoso
5. Grandioso
6. Grave
7. Langsam
8. Larghetto
9. Lebhaft
10. Leggero
11. Lent
12. Marziale
13. Mesto
14. Rasch
15. Più mosso
16. Pizzicato
17. Saltando
18. Senza sordino
19. Stretto
20. Stringendo
21. Sul ponticello
22. Trionfante
23. Vite
24. Vivacissimo
25.

C3 MUSICAL TERMS AND SIGNS ANSWERS

Test 1

1. Broadening
2. At a moderate walking pace
3. Bowed (normally)
4. Animated
5. Sparkling
6. Dying away/getting slower
7. With the wood of the bow
8. With the mute
9. Sweetly
10. Twice as fast
11. Heroically
12. Merrily/joyfully
13. Mournfully
14. Very slowly
15. Moderately
16. Less movement
17. Less fast
18. Dying (away)
19. Heavily
20. Hurrying
21. Fast
22. Sustained
23. Bouncing the bow
24. Lively
25. Measured semiquavers (16th notes)

Test 2

1. Agitated
2. Boldly
3. In a singing style
4. Joyfully/merrily
5. Grandly
6. Slow and solemn
7. Slowly
8. Rather broadly
9. Lively
10. Lightly
11. Slowly
12. Like a march
13. Sadly
14. Quickly
15. More movement
16. Pluck the strings
17. Jumping
18. Without the mute
19. In a faster tempo
20. Pressing on faster
21. Play on the bridge
22. Triumphantly
23. Fast
24. Very fast and lively
25. Glissando (or portamento) – rapidly play all the notes between the two notated.

C4 COMMENTING ON MUSIC

Comparing and contrasting music is a very useful skill, which will help you to convey the nuances of any music you are performing - it shouldn't be just a theoretical exercise.

In the ABRSM grade 6 theory exam, you might be asked to compare two short sections of the same score, and to comment on

- any similarities or differences, **or**
- how the composer has changed the mood of the piece

a) Similarities and Differences

If you are asked to name the similarities or differences between two sections of a score, the sections will normally look quite similar at first glance. You need to look very closely at:

- the rhythm
- the melody
- the dynamics
- the phrasing or articulation
- the instrumentation

Here are some questions you should ask yourself:

- **Rhythm.** Is the rhythm exactly the same, or have the note values changed?
- **Melody.** Has the melody been inverted (turned upside down)? Has it been transposed into a different octave? Has it been sequenced (moved up or down by steps of the scale)?
- **Dynamics.** Are both sections at the same dynamic, or are they contrasted?
- **Phrasing and Articulation.** Are both sections legato, or perhaps one is staccato? Does one section use accented notes, or any other special effects?
- **Instrumentation.** In an orchestral score, the exact same melody/rhythm might be played on a different instrument – has the instrumentation changed?

On the following page is the opening of the fourth movement of Brahms' 1st clarinet sonata. (Can you work out which type of clarinet it is written for?!)

Look at the clarinet part in bars 4-5 and 6-7. What similarities or differences can you see?

- The rhythm is the same.
- The melody is the same but written an octave lower in bars 6-7.
- The dynamics are contrasted – F then P.
- The articulation is the same.

(This is for clarinet in Bb – the clarinet part is written a major second higher than the piano part.)

b) Changing the Mood

If the composer has changed the mood of the piece, he/she has probably changed quite a few of the elements we discussed in point a). A mood change can be from racing to plodding, jolly to melancholic, blaring to peaceful or joking to serious. How does a composer achieve this?

- **Tempo.** Has the composer written a new tempo direction? Has the time signature changed?
- **Dynamics.** Has the composer used different dynamic markings, or fewer instruments to achieve a change in volume?

- **Rhythm and melody.** Has the composer started using longer/shorter note values, or made the melody go a lot higher/lower? The general note range of a melody is called its "tessitura". You can say the "tessitura has become higher", for example.

- **Texture.** Has the composer changed which instruments are playing? The word "texture" refers to the thickness of sound. A full orchestra with all instruments playing has a thick or heavy texture. If this is reduced to just the strings, the texture is thinner or lighter.

- **Modality.** Has the key of the music changed from major to minor?

- **Articulation.** Has the composer changed from a smooth legato to a spiky staccato?

On the following pages is an extract from a Menuet by d'Indy. The change of mood is easy to spot with the double bar lines showing the start of the new section.

How has the composer created the change of mood though? The piece is orchestrated for flute, oboe, clarinet, horn, bassoon and piano.

- The tempo is a little slower.
- The dynamics are slightly quieter.
- The rhythm is built of longer note values (crotchets and minims (half and quarter notes), compared to quavers and semiquavers (8th and 16th notes)).
- The texture is lighter because not all the instruments are playing at the same time.
- The key has changed (to Bb major).
- The articulation has changed from tongued/staccato to legato.

The overall effect would be that the mood has changed to a calmer, more sedate feeling.

C4 COMMENTING ON MUSIC EXERCISES

a. Rameau

Here are bars 9-16 of Rameau's Piano Minuet in A minor – this is the middle section of the piece. Comment on the similarities and differences between bars 9-12 and bars 13-16.

b. Handel

Here are bars 1-5 and bars 45-48 of Handel's Allegro in C (for piano). Comment on the similarities and differences between the two sections.

c. Mozart

This is part of Mozart's Clarinet Quintet. The double bar line in the middle bar 32 signals a change of section. Comment on how the composer achieves a change in mood after the double bar line.

d. Brahms

On the next two pages is part of Brahms' 4th Symphony, bars 133-140 of the first movement. Comment on how the composer changes the mood of the piece at around the end of bar 136.

C4 COMMENTING ON MUSIC ANSWERS

a.

Similarities: the rhythm is the same, bars 13-16 are a melodic sequence of bars 9-12, the phrasing is the same, both sections end with a diminuendo.

Differences: the melody is one scale step lower, the dynamics are contrasted mf, then mp.

b.

Similarities: the rhythm, dynamics and phrasing are the same, part of the melody is the same.

Differences: the melody is raised by an octave in bar 46 and then continues at a higher tessitura ("tessitura" means "pitch range").

c.

The overall dynamic is quieter (no forte sections), the melody is less lyrical/smooth and more spiky/detached, the texture is lighter because the clarinet is now tacit (not playing), the key has changed from major to minor. The mood has changed from light and lyrical to dark and anguished.

d.

The note values are longer, making the melody appear to be slower, the dynamics are much quieter, the texture is lighter with less brass playing, the music is beginning to modulate, and the articulation has mostly changed from staccato to legato. The effect is that the music has lost some energy and become calmer.

C5 KEY
KEY AND MODULATION

The subject of key is discussed in depth in the grade 6 composition course.

In particular, we looked at how to determine what key the **start** of a melody is in. We saw that the primary chords, I and V (or i and V in a minor key) are the most important chords because they help to fix the key.

When you are presented with a score in the grade six music theory exam, you might be asked to determine the key at **any point** in the score. There are three basic ideas to bear in mind:

- The key that the piece **starts** in is its main key. The piece is "in" that key. The piece will **end** in the same key.

- The music might **modulate** to another key. A modulation is a key change which is substantial, settled and lasting. It lasts for several bars and may or may not be accompanied by an actual change of key signature. Modulations often happen when the mood of a piece changes, or a new section is started. With a modulation, a new tonic is established.
When a modulation occurs without an actual change of key signature, we can describe the new key as the "**prevailing key**".

- The music might **pass through** any number of keys. If a key is "passed through", it is only touched upon for a very short time – just a few bars or less, for example. It is not "settled" – we don't get the feeling that a new tonic has been established. Instead, we feel that the key of the music is in transition, moving somewhere else. A piece of music might "pass through" one or more keys before reaching a "modulation".

At whatever point in the score you are trying to work out what the key is, remember that

- a key is most often established with a **dominant-tonic** relationship (look for chords V-I)
- Chord V7 (V with an added 7th above the root) is often used in place of V

This means that you need to:

- look carefully at the **supporting harmony** (don't rely on the melody alone!)
- make a note of which chords are used (e.g. D major, G minor…)
- find the key which has those chords as I and V (the chords should be next to each other).
- if more than one key uses those chords, look at the other melody notes for more clues.

Let's look at a real life example. This is from a flute sonata by Donizetti. Let's try to answer these questions.

- What key does the piece start in?
- What key has it modulated to by bar 16?

- **The piece starts in C minor.**
    - The first chord is C minor, which is i in C minor (a primary chord), but vi in Eb major (not a primary chord), which rules out Eb major.
    - Bar 3 contains nothing but Gs. Since G is the dominant in C minor, this bar would be chord V in C minor.
    - Up until bar 11, we see a lot of B naturals, as would be expected in C minor (the 7th degree of the scale is raised).
- **The piece modulates to Eb major by bar 16.**
    - The modulation starts in bar 14 with the introduction of B flat instead of B natural. The notes of the piano chords are Bb-D-F-Ab, which is chord V7 in Eb major. (It would be chord VII7 in C minor – the major chord formed in that key by *not* raising the 7th degree of the scale).
    - In bar 16, the Eb major chord is stated as the new tonic – the music has modulated to the relative major key of Eb major. (See the next unit for more on "7" chords).
    - In bars 17 and 18, the E natural and F sharp notes are **chromatic passing notes**. They don't affect the key of the piece as they are just a form of melodic decoration. (See the unit on melodic decoration in part A for more on this).
- To sum up, this piece is **in** C minor then **modulates** to the relative major key of Eb.

Tips for Working out Modulations

Although it's possible to modulate to any other key from any starting key, in practice, there are only a small number of **likely modulations**, especially in Baroque and Classical music. These are:

- Tonic to dominant
- Tonic to subdominant
- To relative minor/major

It is usually worth assuming that the modulation is one of these, and then testing out which one it is by looking at the underlying harmony.

You should also scan the score for **accidentals,** then work out which keys those accidentals belong to. In the Donizetti piece above, the B naturals at the start were a clue that the piece starts in C minor. This means you should keep on looking at B's to see when the naturals **stop being used**. Another example could be a piece which starts in C major, but then F#s are introduced - this should lead you to the fact that the likely modulation is to the dominant, G major.

Don't rely on accidentals blindly though. As in the above piece, they are often used simply for decoration. Accidentals which are used for **chromatic melodic decoration** will not affect the key.

AWKWARD KEY QUESTIONS

When working out the key or modulations of a piece of music, don't forget that sometimes you will have to transpose parts (or read awkward clefs) to work out what notes are being played. It can be confusing to work out the key of an orchestral piece, so let's have a go!

On the next page is the beginning of the slow movement of Brahms' 2nd symphony.

- First look at the key signatures here – it's easier to check the key signature of the **non-transposing** instruments to get started. Here, the non-transposing instruments (e.g. violin, flute, oboe, cello…) have five sharps – so is it B major or G# minor?

- Next look at the notes played by the **low-pitched** instruments. Usually, the lower pitched instruments will provide a **bass line** which will help us determine the chords.

  The double bass and bass tuba both have long F#s – sustained (or repeated) notes are always useful when working out key. The cello and bassoon, on the other hand, have a fragment of a melody. Melodies are less useful for determining the key.

  In this case, the double bass and tuba look like good candidates for showing us what the key is, so we will focus on them.

  The next notes played by the double bass and bass tuba are D# and B. Clearly, the piece is in B major, not G# minor. Why? Because F# is the root of the dominant (V) of B major, and D#/B are part of the tonic triad (I). (In G# minor, F# is the root of the **un**raised 7th degree of the scale (VII), which is never a likely chord for the opening of a piece.) Remember: always look for the **V-I** relationship.

- Always look for the parts which move **slowly** or by **leaps** (i.e. intervals larger than a 2nd) – these are likely to be the parts which are providing the **harmony**.
  Parts which move mostly **quickly** or by **step**, are more likely to be supplying the **melody**. We need to analyse the **harmony** of a piece to determine its key.

C5 KEY EXERCISES

Exercise 1

Look at the following 8-bar piano piece and answer the questions below.

a. Which two keys are represented by this key signature?

b. Label the chords in bars 1 and 2 using Roman numerals (e.g. I, ii) in both of these keys.

c. Which of the two keys uses mostly chords I and V?

d. What key does the piece start in and why?

e. Which accidental is introduced in bars 4-5?

f. Which scale uses the sharp in the key signature plus this new accidental?

g. Label the chords in bars 4-6 using Roman numerals in this new key.

h. What is the relationship between the opening key and this new key? (e.g. tonic-dominant, relative major/minor etc.)

i. Which accidentals are used in bars 7-8?

j. Complete the notes used in bars 7-8 in ascending order, starting from B. What key is this scale and which note is missing?

k. Label the chords in bars 7-8 in this new key.

l. What is the relationship between the key used in bars 3-6 and the key used in bars 7-8?

m. Complete the following analysis of the key of the piece: This piece starts in _____, passes through _____ and finally modulates to _____.

EXERCISE 2

Analyse the keys used in the following excerpts. Ask yourself the same kind of questions as you saw in exercise 1 to help you:

- Which keys use these sharps/flats?
- Do these notes belong to chords I (or i) and V or to more "obscure" chords?
- Do these notes make up most of any particular scale?
- Is this new key closely connected to the previous key? (Close relationships are Tonic-Dominant, Tonic-Subdominant and Relative Major - Minor)

a. Schumann - Soldier's March, for piano

This piece starts in _____, and modulates to _____.

b. Pergolesi - Allegro from Sonata no.7 in E, for piano

This piece starts in _____, and modulates to _____.

c. Saint Saëns - Oboe Sonata, First movement (2 pages).

183

This excerpt starts in _____, at bar 14 passes briefly through _____ and then modulates to _____ by the end.

d. Beethoven - Symphony no.1, First movement bars 13-26 (Allegro con Brio section) (2 pages).

This section starts in _____, and modulates to _____ after about 6 bars. The chord in bars 25-26 is the dominant 7th chord in the key of _____.

C5 KEY ANSWERS

Exercise 1

a. G major and E minor.

b. In G major: I-V-I-I ii-ii-V; in E minor: III-VII-III-III iv-iv-VII.

c. G major.

d. G major. Chords I and V are always used to fix the key.

e. D#

f. E minor harmonic

g. Bar 4: V-iv-V; Bar 5: i-V-i-i; Bar 6; iv-iv-i

h. Relative major and minor.

i. C#, A# and D#.

j. B major, with G# missing.

k. Bar 7: V-I-V7; Bar 8: I-I

l. Tonic-dominant.

m. This piece starts in <u>G major</u> passes through <u>E minor</u> and finally modulates to <u>B major</u>.

Exercise 2

a. This piece starts in <u>G major</u> and modulates to <u>D major</u>.

b. This piece starts in <u>E major</u>, and modulates to <u>B major</u>.

c. This excerpt starts in <u>D major</u> passes briefly through <u>B minor</u> and then modulates to <u>E minor</u>.

d. This section starts in <u>C major</u> and modulates to <u>D minor</u> after about 6 bars. The chord in bars 25-26 is the dominant 7th (V7) chord in the key of <u>C major</u>.

C6A NAMING CHORDS

In the ABRSM grade six music theory exam, you will probably be asked to identify a chord or two. This might be in a piano score, or it could be part of a larger ensemble, in which case the notes you need to focus on are usually pinpointed for you.

You'll be asked to identify the chord by **name**, state its **position**, say whether it is **major, minor, augmented** or **diminished**, and you may also have to name the **prevailing key** (see Lesson 5 on Key).

Don't forget to double check the **key signature** and **clef** of any instruments used in the chord. If one of the instruments is a transposing instrument, you'll need to work out what note is actually sounding at **concert pitch**.

In this section of the exam, you might come across **seventh** chords. We will discuss these in a moment. First though, let's revise the basics of chords.

CHORD NAMES

Chords can be named in three basic ways.

1. By **letter name**, e.g. "C major".

    - The four types of chord built from basic triads are **major, minor, augmented** and **diminished**.

2. By **Roman numeral** e.g. I or i.

    - In order to use the Roman numeral system, you need to know what the **prevailing key** of the music is. The prevailing key is the key **at that point** in the music, and not necessarily the key that the piece is "in" overall.
    - Capital letters are used for major chords, and lower case letters for minor chords.
    - Augmented chords are written in capital letters with the symbol + (e.g. III+) and diminished chords are written in lower case with the symbol ° (e.g. vii°).

3. By **technical name** e.g. "dominant" or "diminished supertonic". The technical names of the degrees of the scale are:

    - Tonic (1st)
    - Supertonic (2nd)
    - Mediant (3rd)
    - Subdominant (4th)
    - Dominant (5th)
    - Submediant (6th)
    - Leading note (7th)

Again, you need to know the **prevailing key** of the music in order to use this system.

Major, Minor, Diminished, Augmented and Seventh Chords

Chords with Three Notes

Chords which have **three** different notes in them can be major, minor, augmented or diminished.

To find out what type of chord you've got, put the notes together as closely as you can – you should have three notes which are a **third** apart – a triad.

For example, this score has a chord built with four notes, but only three of them are different.

The cello has C#, the viola has A, the second violin has E, and the first violin has A. This means we have three notes: C#, A and E. If we stack them in thirds, they look like this:

The **bottom** note is the chord's name – this is a chord of A.

Next, calculate the exact interval between the lowest and middle, and then middle and top notes. Each will be either a major third (4 semitones/half steps) or a minor third (3 semitones/half steps).

For example, A-C# is a **major** third. C# to E is a **minor** third. The pattern **major+minor** means the chord is a **major** chord. There are four possible patterns of triads:

- Major+minor=major chord
- Minor+major=minor chord
- Major+major=augmented chord
- Minor+minor=diminished chord

Augmented and diminished chords get their names from the interval made between the root and the 5th of the triad.

Here are some examples.

G-B-D# is an augmented triad, because G-D# is an augmented 5th. Similarly, G-Bb-Db is a diminished triad, because G-Db is a diminished 5th.

Chords with Four Notes

If there are **four** different notes in the chord (in the grade 6 exam), it will be a triad **plus the seventh** – the note which is an interval of a minor seventh above the root (the root is the lowest note).

In the grade six music theory exam, seventh chords are restricted to the **dominant seventh** and the **supertonic seventh** (in major and minor keys).

- In chord 1, the key is C major. The dominant chord in C (chord V) is G major. The note which is a minor seventh above G is F. So, G major plus F is the **dominant 7th of C major**.

- In chord 3, the key is A minor. The dominant is E major, and D is a minor 7th above E. So E major plus D is the **dominant 7th of A minor**.

Notice that dominant 7th chords are always built on a **major** triad, even when in a minor key. This is because the leading note is raised.

INVERSIONS

All chords can be **inverted**. Three-note chords have three possible positions:

- Root position (or "a")
- First inversion ("b")
- Second inversion ("c")

Look at the **lowest** note of the triad. This is the bass note.

If there are several instruments playing the chord, you'll need to look carefully to see which one has the lowest note - don't forget about instruments which sound an octave lower than written, such as the double bass and bass clarinet, and watch out for transposing instruments.

Find out whether the bass note is the **root**, **third** or **fifth** of the chord.

- The root is the fundamental of the triad. Root in bass = **root position "a"**
- The third is a third higher than the root. Third in bass = **first inversion "b"**
- The fifth is a fifth higher than the root. Fifth in bass = **second inversion "c"**

Chords with four notes have four possible inversions:

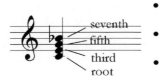

- Root in bass = root position ("a")
- Third in bass = first inversion ("b")
- Fifth in bass = second inversion ("c")
- Seventh in bass = third inversion ("d")

C6B CHORDS IN A SCORE

Let's now look at some real life examples of chords in scores.

This is a chord from Mendelssohn's "A Midsummer Night's Dream", played by the woodwind and horn.

We will examine the chord marked by the box.

The prevailing key is B major. (You need to see a bit more of the score to work that out for yourself, so just take our word for it this time!)

First, write down the letter names of all the notes which are sounding (at concert pitch).

The **flute** and **bassoon** parts are easy in this extract. Generally flute parts will always be easy, but make sure you are comfortable reading the tenor clef for bassoon parts. Bassoon parts often switch clef (from bass to tenor in most cases), so watch out!

There is no **oboe** contribution in this extract. Oboes are easy instruments (to read, not play!) too, as they also play at concert pitch.

The **clarinet** part is a little harder. Clarinets come in many sizes, with the Bb, A and Eb being the most common. It's not unknown to find a part for clarinet in C (i.e. non-transposing) either. In this case, we know that the clarinet must be a transposing instrument, because it's using a **different** key signature. But is it a clarinet in A, Bb or something else?

Start by looking at the key signatures in use. The clarinet is using a key signature of G major, whereas the non-transposing instruments have E major. This means the written notes are a **minor third higher** than they sound (because E-G is a minor third). So, a written G in the clarinet part equals a concert pitch E. All the notes in the clarinet part sound a minor third **lower** than written.

Make sure you understand this concept, because sometimes the excerpts don't mention which kind of clarinet is being used, and with instruments like the cor Anglais the transposing pitch is not usually written because it's always the same (cors Anglais are always in F).

You can also remember the phrase "C that you see = concert pitch key" to help you.

For example:

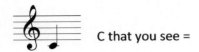 C that you see =

- concert pitch Bb on the Bb clarinet
- concert pitch F on the horn in F
- concert pitch D on the trumpet in D
- etc.

The **horn** part is also transposed. Here, you are told that the horn is in E. You will always be told the specific transposition for a horn or trumpet part, because, traditionally, brass parts are often written with **no key signature**. Because C (horn part) = E (concert pitch), you need to transpose the notes **up** a major third. The written G is a concert pitch B.

With brass instruments, you can't work out the transposition from the key signature (as was done with the clarinet above) if the key signature is left out.

So, these are the notes for each instrument at concert pitch:

- Flutes: B, D#
- Clarinets: B, F#
- Bassoons (Fag.): D#, F#
- Horns (Cor): B, B

We have the notes B, F# and D#. Stacked as closely as possible in thirds, they make the triad of B major.

The lowest note is in the bassoon part – F# (the 5th of the triad). Therefore, this is a second inversion chord.

The full description is: "Tonic chord of B major (I) in the second inversion."

Here's another chord from later in the same piece, this time played by the string section:

This time, we have enough of the score to be able to work out the prevailing key as well. The key signature of two flats means we should start by assuming the key is either Bb major or G minor.

The double bass plays G-D-G-D in the first two bars, which would be the root of the tonic and dominant triads in **G minor** (G minor and D major). In the fourth bar however, **B natural** and **A flat** are introduced – and they appear again in the 6th bar. In the 7th bar there is an **A natural** (no accidental). If we look at the notes in use (from the 4th-7th bars) and lay them out in order, they are Ab-A-B-C-D-Eb-F-G.

These are all notes from the C minor melodic scale. The Ab appears in the descending scale, and the A natural and B natural are in the ascending scale. At this point, the **prevailing key** of the music is C minor.

Next, work out the notes of the chord. They are C, Eb and G. These are the notes of the tonic chord (i) in C minor.

Finally, we check the lowest note of the chord, to work out what position it's in. Don't forget that double basses are transposing instruments **at the octave**, so the note you see written actually sounds an octave lower. (It doesn't make any difference here, because it's the lowest notated note anyway, but that isn't always the case). The lowest note of the chord is Eb, which is the third of the chord. So, this chord is a "tonic, first inversion minor chord in the prevailing key of C minor".

As you can see, identifying chords at this level requires knowing more than just how chords work. Make sure you are super confident about:

- which instruments transpose and at what interval
- reading the alto and tenor clefs
- working out the prevailing key

Get into the habit of working out all the key changes in music that you are actually playing. Practice makes perfect!

C6 NAMING CHORDS EXERCISES

Exercise 1

Name each of the following chords with Roman numeral notation, including the inversion, e.g. Ia (=major chord root position) or ii°b (= diminished chord first inversion), and name the key (major or minor is given).

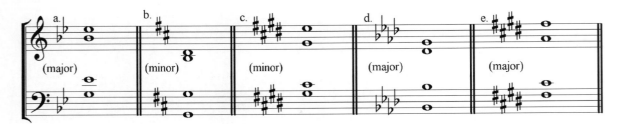

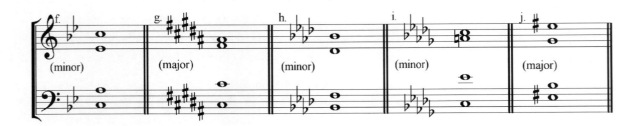

Exercise 2

Work out the key of this Bach Chorale, then describe the lettered chords using the Roman numeral system, including the inversion.

Key:

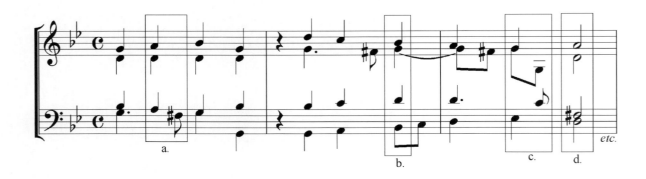

Exercise 3

In this Chorale extract, Bach modulates three times. What key does it start in, when does it modulate and to which other keys?

Starting key:

1st modulation:

2nd modulation:

3rd modulation:

Describe the lettered chords and state the **prevailing key** for each one.

Exercise 4

Look at the extract on the next two pages, which is the beginning of Mozart's 40th Symphony, 3rd Movement.

Using Roman numerals, name the chords marked by the boxes, including their inversions, and state the **prevailing key**. (Remember to include all chord notes which are sounding at that point in the music, but ignore any passing notes.)

C6 NAMING CHORDS ANSWERS

Exercise 1

a. Bb major, IVb

b. B minor, VIa

c. C# minor, ic

d. Ab major, vii°b

e. E major, iia

f. G minor, ii°b

g. B major, Vc

h. F minor, iva

i. Bb minor, vii°b

j. G major, via

Exercise 2

Key: G minor

a. Vb

b. ib

c. ivb

d. Va

Exercise 3

Starting key: A major

1st modulation: first pause, E major

2nd modulation: second pause, A major

3rd modulation: third pause, B minor

a. Ib (prevailing key A major)

b. Va (prevailing key A major)

c. vii°b (prevailing key E major)

d. iiia (prevailing key A major)

e. ib (prevailing key B minor)

f. Va (prevailing key B minor)

Exercise 4

a. ic, prev. key G minor. (Chord notes G-Bb-D with D in the bass)

b. V7d, prev. key G minor. (Chord notes D-F#-A-C with C in the bass)

c. V7b, prev. key G minor. (Chord notes D-F#-A-C with F# in the bass)

d. VIa, prev. key G minor. (Chord notes Eb-G-Bb with Eb in the bass)

e. V7b, prev. key D minor. (Chord notes A-C#-E-G with C# in the bass)

f. ii°b, prev. key D minor. (Chord notes E-G-Bb with G in the bass)

g. VIa, prev. key D minor. (Chord notes Bb-D-F with Bb in the bass)

h. ia, prev. key D minor. (Chord notes D-F-A with D in the bass)

C7A ORNAMENTS

You need to know the same ornaments as you learnt for grade five music theory. The added twist for grade six is that you also have to be able to write them out in full, as they would be played.

Ornament symbols were added to music for several reasons. They allow some freedom of interpretation, and they allow the basic harmony of the music to be more visible.

We'll examine each ornament in turn.

Note that if there is a small accidental written with the ornament, you'll need to add that accidental when the ornament is written out in full too. (See the turn for an example).

The Trill

The trill (or "shake") is a rapid alternation between the note written (called the "principal" note), and the note above. Trills can be very tricky to write out indeed, as the way they are interpreted has always been very subjective and the rules have changed over time. Try to keep to the following basic rules, however:

- The trill can **start** on the note itself or the note above. In earlier music (up to about 1800) the trill usually started on the note above, after 1800 it starts on the note itself.

- The trill is most often written out in **semiquavers or demisemiquavers (16th or 32nd notes)**. The number of notes you need depends on the length of the written note. For example, a crotchet (quarter note) will need 8 demisemiquavers (32nd notes).

- Beam the demisemiquavers (32nd notes) in subdivisions of fours, to make them easier on the eye (see the first example below).

- Sometimes a trill is preceded by an acciaccatura – this means you should start the trill on the acciaccatura note.

- The trill should end on the principal note. This means you might have to add a triplet figure at the end.

In this first example, the trill starts on the higher note because it is (imaginary) Bach (pre-1800).

In this later (fictitious) example (Mendelssohn was born in 1809), the trill starts on the principal note. A triplet is added at the end, so that the trill also finishes on the principal note.

The Turn

The turn consists of four notes: the note above, the principal note, the note below, the principal note again.

- Turns can be performed **after** the written note, or **instead** of it, depending on where they are written. A turn written directly above a note replaces that note. A turn written after the note should be performed after the note is sounded.
- Turns can be written using any note value which is basically **fast**.

The first example here is from a piano Sonata by Beethoven. The turn is written after the note, so we play the Bb first, then the turn.

It can be tricky working out what values to write for each note. The Bb is a dotted quaver (dotted 8th note), and we need to squeeze five notes into the same space.

We can break it down into three semiquavers (16th notes), then put a triplet into the middle semiquaver (16th note) beat.

The next example comes later in the same piece. This time the turn is directly above the note, so it starts on the C.

In this case, the four notes of the turn are divided equally into the semiquaver (16th note) beat.

The Mordent

There are two kinds of mordent – the **lower** mordent, and the **upper** mordent. The mordent consists of three notes.

The lower mordent consists of the principal note, then the note below, then the principal again.

The upper mordent is the same pattern, but using the note above the principal.

Here are some general guidelines:

- The ornament starts on the beat itself (not after)
- The first two notes are played very quickly, and the third note is sustained for longer.
- The lower mordent symbol has a short line through the middle. (Think "**L**ine=**L**ower").

This bar is taken from an Aria by Handel.

The lower mordent includes an accidental sharp, which means the C must be sharpened. The D is a crotchet (quarter note), so we can give a quarter of its value to the mordent itself, and then have a dotted quaver (dotted 8th) left over for the sustained principal note.

There are no hard and fast rules about what note values to write, but notice here that semiquavers (16th notes) are common in the music already. The mordent should be quicker than any note values already commonly used.

The following upper mordent appears in a Sonatina by Benda (a Czech 18th century violinist and composer). Notice here that the pace is calmer than in the previous example, with quavers and crotchets (8th and quarter notes) in use.

The mordent can be performed with semiquavers (16th notes). Demisemiquavers (32nd notes) would be ok too.

The Acciaccatura

When an acciaccatura is performed, the principal note remains on the beat and the ornament is squeezed in **beforehand**. The ornaments usually consist of just two notes – the "crushed" note and the principal note.

Sometimes, though, you might find two or more notes in an acciaccatura – in which case they will **all** have to be squeezed in before the beat!

- Acciaccaturas are notated with a small-size quaver (8th note) with a slash through the tail.
- Acciaccaturas are performed very quickly.
- As the principal note falls **on** the beat, the acciaccatura has to "steal" its time from the **previous** note.

In this example from a Bagatelle by Beethoven, the acciaccatura F# has to steal some time from the D before it, so that the E quaver (8th note) remains on the beat.

Write the acciaccatura with a semiquaver or demisemiquaver (8th or 16th note), then work out how much of the previous note is left.

The Appoggiatura

An appoggiatura is written with small-size notes. In contrast to the acciaccatura, the appoggiatura falls **on the beat**, not before it.

- An appoggiatura can be one or more notes.
- The notation of the appoggiatura shows you which note length to use.
- The appoggiatura does **not** have a slash through its tail.

In this example, from an Allegro by Pergolesi (an 18th century Italian composer), the appoggiatura is notated with a quaver (8th note).

We use the same value when writing it out, and reduce the following G to a quaver (8th note) too.

C7A ORNAMENTS EXERCISES

1. Composer: John Blow (1648-1708)

a) What kind of ornament is this?

b) Which note should it start on and why?

c) Write out the ornament as it should be played

2. Composer: Carl Czerny (1791-1857)

a) What kind of ornament is this?

b) Which note should it start on and why?

c) Write out the ornament as it should be played

3. Composer: Joseph Haydn (1732-1809)

a) What kind of ornament is this?

b) Which notes is it made up of?

c) Write out the ornament as it should be played

4. Composer: Carl Maria von Weber (1786-1826)

a) What kind of ornament is this?

b) Does it begin **off** or **on** the beat?

c) Write out the ornament as it should be played

5. Composer: JS Bach (1685-1750)

a) What kind of ornament is this?

b) Which notes is it made up of?

c) Write out the ornament as it should be played

6. Composer: Casella (1883-1947)

a) What kind of ornament is this?

b) Does it begin **off** or **on** the beat?

c) Write out the ornament as it should be played

7. Composer: Joseph Haydn (1732-1809)

a) What kind of ornament is this?

b) Which notes is it made up of?

c) Write out the ornament as it should be played

8. Composer: Joseph Haydn (1732-1809)

a) What kind of ornament is this?

b) Which notes is it made up of?

c) Write out the ornament as it should be played

9. Composer: Anton Diabelli (1781-1858)

a) What kind of ornament is this?

b) Which notes is it made up of?

c) Write out the ornament as it should be played

10. Composer: Carl Maria von Weber (1786-1826)

a) What kind of ornament is this?

b) Does it begin **off** or **on** the beat?

c) Write out the ornament as it should be played

11. Composer: Georg Frideric Handel (1685-1759)

a) What kind of ornament is this?

b) Which note should it start on and why?

c) Write out the ornament as it should be played

12. Composer: Georg Frideric Handel (1685-1759)

a) What kind of ornaments are these?

b) Write out the ornaments as they should be played

C7A ORNAMENTS ANSWERS

There are several possible ways to write out most ornaments. The following are example answers. The ABRSM will credit you for writing the correct pitches at a suitable speed, with correct notation.

1a. Trill

1b. The upper note (B), because it's from before 1800.

1c.

2a. Trill

2b. The principal note (B), because it's from after 1800.

2c.

3a. Turn

3b. The note above, the note itself, the note below, the note itself again.

3c.

4a. Appoggiatura

4b. On the beat.

4c.

5a. Lower mordent

5b. The note itself, the note below, the note itself again

5c.

6a. Appoggiatura

6b. On the beat.

6c.

7a. Turn

7b. The note above, the note itself, the note below, the note itself again.

7c.

8a. Upper mordent

8b. The note itself, the note above, the note itself again.

8c.

9a. Turn

9b. The note itself, the note above, the note itself, the note below, the note itself again.

9c.

10a. Acciaccatura

10b. Off the beat.

10c.

11a. Trill

11b. The note above (C), because it's from before 1800.

11c.

12a. Trill and lower mordent.

12b.

C7B MELODIC DECORATION AND PEDALS

Apart from ornaments, melodies can also be "decorated" in other ways. Basically this means using notes which don't exist as part of the supporting chord at that moment in time.

If the harmony has a chord of **G major**, for example, and the melody has an **A,** the A is a "non-chord" tone and is there for **decorative** purposes.

Think of it like this: if the A wasn't there, the underlying harmony would be unchanged. If composers didn't decorate their melodies with non-chord tones, music would be rather boring.

Melodic decoration is covered in depth in the Harmony section of this course. Here is a list of the types of melodic decoration that you might have to spot in a score:

- **Passing note** – accented or unaccented, diatonic or chromatic. A passing note is a note between two chord notes which are a 3rd apart (e.g. the D in c-D-e).

- **Auxiliary note** – accented or unaccented, diatonic or chromatic (also called "neighbour note"). An auxiliary note is a note between two identical notes, which is one scale step away (e.g. the D in c-D-c).

- **Changing note** (including Échappée). A changing note is a note between two chord notes, which is a step away from one, and a leap away from the other in the opposite direction (e.g. the D in c-D-b)

- **Anticipation**. An anticipation is a chord note sounded earlier than the rest of the chord. It is dissonant with the chord it occurs in. (E.g. the note C played against a chord of G major, which is then followed by a C major chord).

- **Suspension**. A suspension is a note held over from a previous chord and dissonant in the chord it sounds with. It resolves downwards.

- **Retardation**. A retardation is a note held over from a previous chord and dissonant in the chord it sounds with. It resolves upwards.

- **Appoggiatura (written out)**. The appoggiatura note creates a dissonance with at least one other note being played at the same time, and it resolves by step either upwards or downwards. The note it resolves onto is consonant (i.e. not dissonant) with the other note being played. Here is an example:

The D (circled) is an appoggiatura, because it is dissonant with the C and E played at the same time. It resolves downwards by step to C, which is a note consonant with the rest of the chord.

- Sometimes an appoggiatura is identical to an accented passing note, such as here:

Now the D is between the notes E and C, so it can be classed as an unaccented passing note as well. However, when the appoggiatura is written with an ornament symbol (see C7a Ornaments) it is always called an appoggiatura, rather than a passing note.

Pedals

A pedal is a note which is repeated or held for some time, while the chord above changes. For example, a tonic pedal might be found in the bass, while the chords in the higher parts change from tonic to supertonic to dominant. The C in the bass clef is the pedal:

- Pedals are also often found on the dominant.
- Pedals can be **inverted**. Usually a pedal is found in the bass, but sometimes it can be found in a **higher part**, in which case it is an "inverted pedal".
- Pedals can be **sustained**. A sustained pedal is a long held note. An unsustained pedal is a repeated note. In the example above, the pedal is not sustained. If we replaced the four crotchets (quarter notes) with a semibreve (whole note), it would be sustained.

C7B MELODIC DECORATION AND PEDALS EXERCISES

Exercise 1

In the following excerpts labelled A, B and C, name each of the following numbered examples of melodic decoration as one of the following:

- Unaccented passing note
- Accented passing note
- Unaccented chromatic passing note
- Accented chromatic passing note
- Auxiliary note (or neighbour note)
- Chromatic auxiliary note (or neighbour note)
- Anticipation
- Suspension
- Retardation
- Changing note (including échappée)

A.

B.

C.

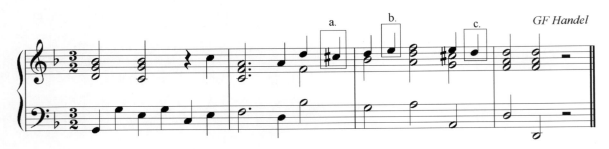

Exercise 2

In the following piece, find an unsustained pedal. Mark its start and end points and say whether it is a tonic or dominant pedal.

C7B MELODIC DECORATION AND PEDALS ANSWERS

Exercise 1

A.

a. Unaccented passing note

b. Auxiliary note

c. Unaccented chromatic passing note

d. Suspension

e. Changing note

f. Accented passing note

B.

a. Unaccented passing note

b. Auxiliary note

c. Chromatic auxiliary note

d. Accented passing note

e. Changing note

C.

a. Chromatic auxiliary note

b. Unaccented passing note

c. Anticipation

Exercise 2

Tonic pedal:

C8 TECHNICAL TASKS

The technical exercises you might be asked to do in your grade six theory exam are basically the same as in grade five – the only difference is that you get less help (i.e. you have to work out more things for yourself), and you have to be comfortable with reading a full orchestral score.

In recent exam papers, the following types of question have come up – here's how they differ from grade five music theory:

- **Transposing a few bars.** In grade five you are told the interval to transpose by to go to or from concert pitch, e.g. the clarinet in Bb should be transposed "down a major 2nd". At grade six, you need to work out the interval and direction by yourself.

- **Rewriting in a new time signature.** At grade six, you'll need to locate the section of the score yourself, then work out how to change the time to compound/simple without changing the rhythmic effect.

- **Intervals.** As in grade five, you need to be able to name any interval in any key, as major, minor, perfect, augmented or diminished. At grade six, you might first have to transpose notes to concert pitch to work out the interval, you'll need to know which are the transposing instruments, and be able to read all four clefs. You might get a harmonic (vertical) interval which encompasses two different instruments on different staves, using two different clefs, playing at two different transpositions!

TRANSPOSITION

Here's an extract from the Largo from Dvořák's "New World Symphony".

How would you write out the cor Anglais part at concert pitch?

You might remember that cors Anglais are pitched in F.

If you've forgotten that, you could look at the key signature of the cor Anglais (4 flats=Ab major), and then compare it to the violins (5 flats=Db major). Db is a perfect 5th lower than Ab, so we will transpose the part **down a perfect 5th**.

Here are the first four bars:

INTERVALS

How would you work out the harmonic intervals marked A-D in the same score?

- Start by double checking the clef, key signature and transposition of each instrument.
- Mark down each note as it sounds **at concert pitch** on a scrap of manuscript paper.
- Be sure to write each note in the correct octave - you will need to know where **middle C** is for each clef.
- Then work out the interval in the normal way.

Intervals are covered in depth in the grade 5 course book.

*As a quick review: take the lower note in the interval to be the **tonic** of a **major** scale. If the upper note is also in the same major scale, the interval must be **perfect** (unison, 4th, 5th or octave) or **major** (2nd, 3rd, 6th or 7th). If the upper note is **not** in the same major scale, the interval must be minor, diminished or augmented. A **minor** interval is one semitone smaller than a major interval. Only 2nds, 3rds, 6ths and 7ths can be minor. A **diminished** interval is one semitone smaller than a minor or perfect interval. An **augmented** interval is one semitone larger than a major or perfect interval. A **compound** interval is larger than one octave – a "9th" is the same thing as a "compound 2nd".*

A: Major 3rd

B: Major 10th (or compound major 3rd)

C: Perfect 5th

D: Perfect 5th

REWRITING IN A NEW TIME SIGNATURE

A little later in the same piece, the flutes have the following passage:

How would you write out the passage, keeping the rhythm the same but using a **compound** time signature?

Remember that with a simple time signature, there are X number of plain beats per bar, (X is the top number of the time signature). In a compound time signature, you keep the same number of beats, but make them **dotted**.

So instead of having four plain crotchets (quarter notes) per bar, we need four dotted crotchets (dotted quarter notes), which means the new time signature will be 12/8.

Here is the answer:

Notice the use of duplets and tuplets.

- "Duplets" are used when two notes are sounded in the space of three. Duplets use the number "2".
- "Triplets" are used when three notes are sounded in the space of two. Triplets use the number "3".
- "Tuplets" can be of any number – just write the number of notes (of the same value) you've got, which replace whatever the usual number should be.
- Duplets, triplets and tuplets should be beamed together, or bracketed if there are no beams.

C8 TECHNICAL TASKS EXERCISES

Exercise 1

Give the **interval** and **direction** of transposition needed for these instruments to create concert pitch (e.g. "up a major 2nd"):

a) Clarinet in Bb

b) cor Anglais

c) French horn in F

d) Clarinet in A

e) Double bass

f) Clarinet in Eb

Exercise 2

Look at the score below and on the next page, which is adapted from a clarinet quintet by Franz Krommer, then answer the questions below it.

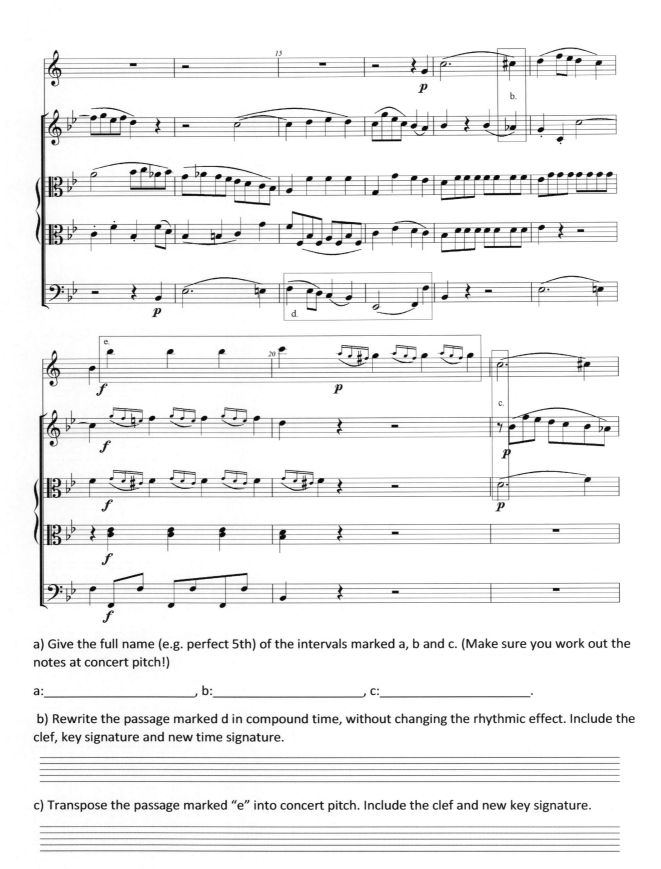

a) Give the full name (e.g. perfect 5th) of the intervals marked a, b and c. (Make sure you work out the notes at concert pitch!)

a:_____, b:_____, c:_____.

b) Rewrite the passage marked d in compound time, without changing the rhythmic effect. Include the clef, key signature and new time signature.

c) Transpose the passage marked "e" into concert pitch. Include the clef and new key signature.

Exercise 3

Look at this score (continues on the next page) which is part of the second movement of the "Symphony Fantastique" by Hector Berlioz, then answer the questions below.

a) Give the full name (e.g. perfect 5th) of the intervals marked a (bar 35, 2nd flute & clarinet), b (bar 39, violas) and c (bar 40, clarinet & horn).

A: _____, b: _____, c: _____.

b. Transpose the passage marked d (French horn part, bars 36- 39) into concert pitch. Include the clef and new key signature.

c. This passage is in 6/8 time. Rewrite the bars marked e in simple time, without changing the rhythmic effect. Include the clef, key signature and new time signature.

Exercise 4

Look at the score on the next page, which is the opening bars of Claude Debussy's "Nuages", then answer the questions below.

a) Give the full names of the intervals marked a (oboe & 1st clarinet), b (2nd clarinet & 1st bassoon) and c (2nd flute and cor Anglais).

A:_____, b:_____, c:_____.

b) Rewrite the passage marked d in simple time, without changing the rhythmic effect. Write out both bassoon parts on one stave and include the new time signature.

c) Transpose the two horn parts marked e as they would sound at concert pitch. Write them on the staves below **without** a key signature.

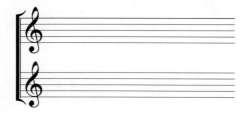

C8 TECHNICAL TASKS ANSWERS

EXERCISE 1

a. Down a major 2nd; b. Down a perfect 5th; c. Down a perfect 5th; d. Down a minor 3rd; e. Down a perfect octave; f. Up a minor 3rd.

EXERCISE 2

a. a) Compound major 3rd or major 10th (viola Eb below violin G). b) Augmented 2nd (violin Ab below clarinet B natural). c) Minor 6th (viola D below clarinet Bb)

b.

c.

EXERCISE 3

a.

a) Compound Major 3rd (or Major 10th) (flute F below clarinet high A). b) Minor 3rd (A below C). c) Perfect octave (horn middle C below clarinet high C).

b.

c.

EXERCISE 4

a.

a) Diminished 4th (clarinet A# below oboe D). b) Perfect 5th (bassoon B below clarinet F#). c) Minor 3rd (cor Anglais E below flute G).

b.

c.

C9 PERIODS AND COMPOSERS

It's likely that you will have to guess the composer or time period of one of the scores in your grade six music theory exam. You will normally have a choice of four, and will sometimes have to give a reason for your choices. The extracts chosen for the exam will always be **typical** of their era – you won't be tricked with a piece which was written in Modern times, but is Classical in style!

You won't need to be able to differentiate between composers of the **same era**. You only need to know which composers are from which era, and what are the characteristics of music from that era, not the individual characteristics of the composers themselves.

Periods

The musical periods are usually broken down into hundred year stretches (in the exam). We can give these periods names:

- 1600-1700 - Baroque
- 1700-1800 - Classical
- 1800-1900 - Romantic
- 1900-2000 - Modern

Note: the musical eras are not generally defined with these specific dates, but it is useful for exam purposes to think of them in this way).

Composers

Some of the most famous composers of each era are as follows:

- **Baroque** – Bach, Purcell, Handel
- **Classical** – Mozart, Schubert, Haydn,
- **Romantic** – Beethoven, Rachmaninov, Elgar, Chopin, Mendelssohn, Dvořák, Wagner, Berlioz, Verdi
- **Modern** – Ravel, Debussy, Ireland, Shostakovich, Gershwin, Britten, Stockhausen

While some composers (e.g. Mozart) were prolific and wrote in many different genres, other composers focused on just a few types of composition. It's useful to know these:

- Chopin & Rachmaninov – piano music, or piano with orchestra
- Strauss – waltzes
- Verdi & Wagner – operatic
- Schubert – Lieder (songs for voice and piano)

The best way to learn about the styles of each of these composers, is to listen to them. Use a website like Youtube, and try to listen critically to a selection of music from each era. Think about the following criteria as you listen:

- Instruments
- Texture
- Harmony
- Expression
- Form

Instruments

You can sometimes easily find a clue to the period by checking what instruments are playing.

- The clarinet did not exist in Baroque times
- Piano music barely existed in Baroque times
- The harpsichord was used in Baroque times but became less popular in later eras

In general, the size of the orchestra was much smaller in Baroque and Classical times, and at its biggest in the Romantic period.

Texture

"Texture" in music refers to the way instruments combine with each other in an ensemble.

In the Baroque era, each instrument/voice was often weighted equally, with separate melodies woven together intricately to make a harmonious sound. Each part would be quite independent. This is called **counterpoint**. We can say the music has a "contrapuntal texture".

The following piece is by Bach (written for "clavier", which means "keyboard instrument"- either the harpsichord or clavichord).

Although it's a composition for just one instrument, Bach uses the contrapuntal style by writing separate strands of music which are interwoven.

The melody begins at A in the right hand. At B, the left hand plays a similar tune, but a fifth lower. At C, a third part is added, playing the same notes as in A, but an octave lower. At this point, the right hand has to play the upper two parts, and the left hand begins the third part.

This type of composition is called a "fugue".

Another common contrapuntal genre from the Baroque period is a vocal composition called the "chorale". The harmonisations and figured bass exercises in the grade six music theory exam are all based on the chorale style.

This is an example by Buxtehude, from his harmonisation of "Wie soll ich dich empfangen", for two sopranos, bass and a "continuo" (keyboard) part. Notice how the voice parts enter one after another, with the same melody (one at an interval of a 5th) in the same way as in the above fugue.

Not all Baroque music was contrapuntal in texture, but if you do see music written like this it's likely that it will have been written by a Baroque composer.

In the Classical era, the texture of music is generally less "complicated" than in the Baroque era. Music of the Classical era tends to sound light, clear and elegant. Instead of being mostly "contrapuntal", at this time music was mostly "homophonic".

Homophonic (which literally means "sounding together") usually means there is a single melody which has an accompaniment based on chords. (Compare this to "contrapuntal" music, which has several melodies woven together.)

Here is part of Mozart's Clarinet Quintet (for clarinet and string quartet). Notice how the melody is almost completely in the clarinet part, with the strings providing an accompaniment.

In the Romantic era, textures became thicker, richer and more luscious. Romantic music is also more likely to feature dramatically contrasted sections – for example a full-on orchestral section followed by just the woodwind and cellos, for example.

Here is another clarinet quintet, this time by Brahms.

Notice how much richer the texture is. Instead of there being a simple melody plus accompaniment, the parts are more involved. The clarinet has the melody, but the first violin imitates it a beat and a half off-set. The second violin, viola and cello have a complicated quaver (8th note)/triplet accompaniment, which will sound much heavier than the crotchets (quarter notes) in the Mozart quintet.

The piece is in 3/4, but rather than having, say, three crotchets (quarter notes) or perhaps six quavers (8th notes) in a bar, there is a huge amount of rhythmic movement going on. In the first bar alone, there are notes being played at 11 different instances - each beat is divided into triplets, but the second two beats are also divided into normal quavers (8th notes). This makes the texture sound **dense**.

Modern era music is not really defined by texture – modern composers tend to be very experimental, and use all kinds of textures.

Harmony

In Baroque and Classical music, pieces were usually written in one key for long stretches. Modulation was usually only to **related keys**, the relative major or minor, the dominant, or occasionally the subdominant.

In Romantic music, composers travelled to more **distant keys** when modulating. They would still employ a pivot chord (a chord which exists in both keys) to propel the music to a new key, but did not feel restricted to closely related keys.

Romantic music tends to use more melodic chromaticism (adding flats or sharps to the music because "it sounds nice", rather than only for modulation purposes).

In Modern music, many composers abandoned the **diatonic** system, which is the system using major and minor scales as a basis for a piece.

Some composers experimented with building pieces based on other types of scale. For example, Debussy exploited the **pentatonic scale** (the 5-note scale you get by playing only the black notes on a piano).

You can explain your choice in the grade six music theory exam by saying the "harmonic language is typical of X era".

EXPRESSION

Each musical era developed organically from the previous one, and there will be overlaps. We can define each era roughly, however, in the following ways.

Baroque music

- Marked with a tempo, ornaments and minimal articulation markings.
- Not usually marked with "expression" directions written in words.
- Dynamics often change abruptly. One section will be soft, the next will be loud, without a crescendo in between.
- The mood of a piece will remain the same throughout.
- Melodies are often long and energetic.

Classical music

- Expression directions are sometimes used, but not heavily.
- Dynamics can be gradual, with long crescendos or decrescendos.
- The mood of a piece can change considerably as the piece progresses.
- Melodies are shorter than in Baroque music.

Romantic music

- Directions for expression are abundant and descriptive, including detailed articulation (staccato, accents, sforzandos, etc.)
- Dynamics change frequently, either gradually or suddenly.
- The mood of a piece is more dramatic – tragedy, comedy or romance, for example.
- Melodies are often more lyrical, song-like.

Modern music

- Expression directions can be incredibly precise and may not be restricted to the "traditional" Italian terms.
- Dynamics may go to extremes or be used for special effects.
- The mood of a piece and types of melody used are completely open to the composer's imagination. They may be **atonal** (not built from notes which correspond to a diatonic or modal scale), **discordant** (jarring chords), **modal** (based on a very old scale system) or something else altogether.

Here's a summary of the clues that can help you answer this question.

Baroque	Classical	Romantic	Modern
Harpsichord ✓ Clarinet × Piano ×	Harpsichord (✓) Clarinet ✓ Piano ✓	Harpsichord × Clarinet ✓ Piano ✓	Harpsichord × Clarinet ✓ Piano ✓
Contrapuntal	Homophonic, light	Homophonic, dense	Anything
Many ornaments	Some ornaments	Few ornaments	Few ornaments
Related modulation	Related modulation	Modulation from pivot	Any modulation
Few chromatics	Some chromatics	Many chromatics	Many chromatics
Usually diatonic, sometimes modal	Always diatonic	Always diatonic	Sometimes diatonic
Mood constant	Mood varies	Moods are dramatic and varied	Anything
Small orchestra	Medium orchestra	Large orchestra	Medium orchestra
Few (de)crescendos	Many (de)crescendos	Many (de)crescendos	Anything
Long, energetic melodies	Short, elegant melodies	Song-like melodies	Anything
Few expression directions	Some expression directions	Many expression directions	Very precise expression directions

In fact, it's rare to find a Modern piece in the grade six music theory exam, although they do crop up from time to time. The main give away that a piece is Modern is that it doesn't conform to any of the other categories, particularly in its harmony.

Although a large number of modern pieces are diatonic, just like in the other eras, in an exam situation you will normally be presented with a non-diatonic piece if it is Modern.

Giving reasons for your choice

If you have to give reasons for your choice of era/composer, you can use some of the following phrases, depending on the extract. (You can replace the words in brackets with whatever is appropriate):

The	harmonic language texture (piano) instrumental combination melodic style use of dynamics	is characteristic of is not characteristic of	(Bach) (Mozart) (Beethoven) (Debussy)
The lack of	ornaments expression marks		

Further help

Quite often the extract you have to identify is from a famous piece of music. The broader your knowledge of music in general, the easier this question will be. Use the free resources around you and try to listen to a wide range of music every day. You could try:

- Tuning in to your local classical radio station (many are online too)
- Watching videos on Youtube.com
- Exploring the free MP3 recordings available via http://www.classiccat.net/ and http://imslp.org/wiki/Main_Page
- Borrowing recordings from your local music library

Take a look at some of the series on the MyMusicTheory blog. Although not aimed at exam students specifically, you will find http://blog.mymusictheory.com/guide-to-music/ useful for revision purposes, and also for further listening.

C9 PERIODS AND COMPOSERS EXERCISES

Exercise 1

Name the musical period which most closely fits with each of these centuries:

a) 1600-1700

b) 1700-1800

c) 1800-1900

d) 1900-2000

Exercise 2

Which musical period does each of these composers belong to?

a) Britten

b) Mozart

c) Elgar

d) Beethoven

e) Handel

f) Ireland

g) Shostakovich

h) Bach

i) Ravel

j) Purcell

k) Haydn

l) Gershwin

m) Verdi

n) Berlioz

o) Debussy

p) Schubert

q) Wagner

r) Stockhausen

Exercise 3

Using the given clues, name the most likely period for each description:

a) A lyrical piece for a big orchestra that modulates from C major to E minor, about a shipwreck.

b) An energetic piece for four instruments each with an independent melody line, entirely in A minor.

c) A piece for two instruments which each have a different key signature and time signature.

d) A song about unrequited love for soprano voice with a wide range of dynamics and a heavy, chordal piano accompaniment.

e) A piece for solo harpsichord with several ornaments such as trills and turns.

f) A piece built on a pentatonic scale which uses several parallel chords such as C major, D major, E major in succession, and is peppered with highly descriptive performance instructions in French.

g) A piece for clarinet and string quartet which comprises an elegant melody against a light, detached, chordal accompaniment.

Exercise 4

Look at the following extracts and name the most likely musical period each one dates from, giving reasons for your choice.

a)

b.

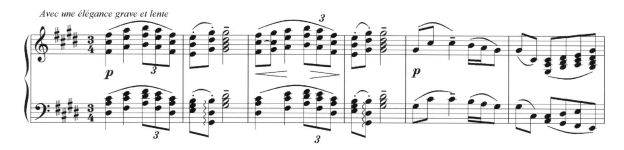

233

c.

d.

e.

f.

g.

h.

i.

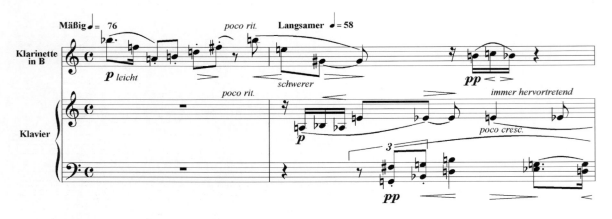

j.

k.

l.

m.

237

C9 PERIODS AND COMPOSERS ANSWERS

Exercise 1

a. Baroque   b. Classical   c. Romantic   d. Modern

Exercise 2

a. Modern   b. Classical   c. Romantic   d. Romantic   e. Baroque   f. Modern   g. Modern

h. Baroque   i. Modern   j. Baroque   k. Classical   l. Modern   m. Romantic   n. Romantic

o. Modern   p. Classical   q. Romantic   r. Modern

Exercise 3

a. Romantic   b. Baroque   c. Modern   d. Romantic   e. Baroque   f. Modern   g. Classical

Exercise 4

a. Romantic (Elgar). Lyrical solo against a complicated accompaniment, use of chromatics, very expressive.

b. Modern (Debussy). Parallel chords, precise French performance directions.

c. Classical (Haydn). Elegant solo against a simple accompaniment, diatonic harmony (not chromatic).

d. Classical (Verdi). Elegant vocal line against simple, chord-based diatonic accompaniment.

e. Baroque (Handel). Baroque instruments, use of imitation, contrapuntal, minimal performance directions.

f. Romantic (Chopin). Lyrical solo, complicated accompaniment, chromatics.

g. Baroque (Bach). Contrapuntal, imitation, lack of performance directions.

h. Modern (Stravinksy). Mixed time signatures, non-diatonic (atonal), many performance directions.

i. Modern (Berg). Highly chromatic, non-diatonic, many performance directions, irregular rhythms.

j. Baroque (Purcell). Contrapuntal, imitation, lack of performance directions.

k. Romantic (Rachmaninov). Many performance directions for dynamics and attack, complicated piano technique, intense mood, thick texture.

l. Classical (Mozart). Diatonic, elegant and simple, modest performance directions with dynamic contrasts, homophonic.

m. Classical (Haydn). Simple, diatonic, some performance directions, elegant, light texture.